Easter Island

Land of Mysteries

illustrated with photographs

Peggy Mann

Easter Island
Land of Mysteries

Holt, Rinehart and Winston / New York

The photographs on pages 2, 17, 70, 84,
108–9, 125, 131, 146, 163, 183, and 196
are by George Holton. All other
photographs are by the author.

Library of Congress Cataloging in Publication Data

Mann, Peggy
Easter Island: land of mysteries.

SUMMARY: Describes the history, culture, and
people of Easter Island from ancient times to the
present day.
1. Easter Island—Juvenile literature.
[1. Easter Island] I. Title.
F3169.M26   996:.18   75-32247
ISBN 0-03-014056-0

Other Books by P E G G Y M A N N

The Last Escape:
*The Launching of the Largest Secret Rescue
Movement of All Time*
Ralph Bunche: *UN Peacemaker*
Luis Muñoz Marín: *The Man who Re-made Puerto Rico*
Golda: *The Life of Israel's Prime Minister*
A Room in Paris
The Telltale Line: *The Secrets of Handwriting Analysis*
A Present for Yanya
The Man Who Bought Himself: *The Story of Peter Still*
Last Road to Safety
Whitney Young, Jr.: *Crusader for Equality*
My Dad Lives in a Downtown Hotel
Amelia Earhart: *First Lady of Flight*
Clara Barton
The Clubhouse
The Street of the Flower Boxes

My deep appreciation for the invaluable help they accorded me in researching this book to:

Gonzalo Figueroa
Lars-Eric Lindblad
Dr. William Mulloy
Gabriel Pakarati
General Roberto Parragué
Alfonso Rapu
Dr. Carlyle S. Smith

For George Holton

Contents

EQUADOR

PERU

Lake Titicaca

BOLIVIA

Copiapo

Valparaiso
Santiago

Juan
Fernandez
Islands

ARGENTINA

CHILE

MARQUESAS

Pacific Ocean

TAHITI

PITCAIRN

EASTER ISLAND

Easter Island: Forty-eight square miles
Surrounded by one million square miles of ocean.

N
W — E
S

Part I

The Discoverers

EASTER ISLAND
(RAPA-NUI)

• Dots indicate coastal Ahus (altars)

Easter Island is about fourteen miles long
and seven miles wide.

N · E · W · S

ANA O KEKE

CAPE ROGGOVEEN

POIKE

La Perouse Bay

POIKE DITCH

RANO RARAKU

RANO RARAKU QUARRY

ANAKENA

RANO AROI

VAITEA

AHU AKIVI

AKAHANGA

VAIHU

ORITO

TAHAI

PUNA PAU QUARRY

HANGA ROA VILLAGE

HANGA PIKO

MATAVERI

VINAPU

HANGA ROA BAY

RANO KAU

ANAKAI TANGATA

ORONGO

MOTU KAOKAO

MOTU ITI

MOTU NUI

For centuries, Easter Island was the most isolated populated spot on earth—a rock-ribbed speck of land surrounded by a million square miles of empty ocean.

Few visitors managed to make their way to this tiny volcanic triangle in the vast Southeast Pacific. But millions journeyed there in stories and dreams. They were drawn by Easter's mysterious population—not the native islanders although they had their own unique fascination, but Easter's amazing population of stone. Almost 1,000 towering statues had been carved by prehistoric men with no tools other than chips of rock. Although the monoliths weighed from five to eighty tons, and some were as tall as a three-story building, they had somehow been transported for miles and then set up on high altars rimming the cliff-bound coast.

Some of the statues were adorned with huge topknots of red sandstone, two to ten tons in weight. How had these massive pieces been lifted into place—a feat which, centuries later, proved difficult even with cranes, cranks, and chains?

And why red topknots, when the statues themselves were hewn from yellow-gray rock? Eighteenth-century seamen who landed on the island noted that not all the natives had black hair. Some had cinnamon-colored locks worn in "topknot style." Did the statuemakers consider redheads to be superior creatures? Was that why their hair color was immortalized in stone?

And why did all of the statues have long ear lobes? Early visitors had also noted that many of the natives had shoulder-length lobes which dangled into the food when a man was eating and, for convenience's sake, had to be tied back. Were long lobes a status symbol—immortalized in the statues?

Who were these long-eared islanders? Where had they come from? What had caused their compulsion for carving the many hundreds of somber, scornful-looking stone giants? And what had suddenly ended it all? Why had each statue been toppled from its alter to lie ignominiously, face in the dirt, throughout the decades?

There were more mysteries.

In every other section of the globe, utter isolation had meant a virtually cultureless savagery. Writing, road building, complex religions, well-organized social systems, construction of monuments had, throughout history, developed in locations that were crossroads of the world; places that people could reach with relative ease; where ideas and knowledge could be interchanged and stimulated to still further growth. The noted American anthropologist Dr. William Mulloy, put it this way:[1]*

> . . . culture is largely a product of idea swapping. Complex civilizations have developed where large populations had out-side contacts, and where advantage could be taken of ideas invented elsewhere. It is no accident that the first civilizations

Recent restoration of a twenty-ton monolith with six-ton topknot, made by Stone Age islanders.

*Numbers refer to Bibliographical Notes at end of book.

developed in southwestern Asia where Africa, Asia, and Europe meet. Conversely, the ultimate simplicity of human life is seen at the ends of the earth among such people as the Alacaluf and the Yahgan of Tierra del Fuego, the Bushmen of the Kalahari Desert, and the Tasmanians. These small groups live where foreign contacts have been rare and the flow of ideas sharply restricted.

At Easter Island during the days of the prehistoric statue-makers, foreign contacts were not only rare, they were nonexistent. The closest land they knew was the moon.

Yet, these remarkable Stone Age men created their own complex culture.

They had a unique hieroglyphic writing; this was the only known writing ever developed in all of Polynesia.

They built wide, paved roads, most of them leading down to the sea.

They understood such celestial happenings as the equinoxes and the solstices—and they put this knowledge to use.

They developed a well-organized political and social structure which enabled all the islanders to live in peace and to produce "public works" which included over 350 *ahus* (altars), some of them 350 feet long, and the momentous stone men who stood upon them.

After pointing out that the island population could never have exceeded three or four thousand people, Dr. Mulloy one of the world's leading Easter Island experts, summed up the scientific reaction to ". . . such hallmarks of cultural complexity. . . . All this on so small and remote an island understandably evokes genuine astonishment."[2]

This astonishment increases when one looks at the island itself. Easter is no Polynesian paradise where people could live merely by plucking fruit from the trees and scooping fish from the sea. Unlike other Polynesian islands, there are no protective coral reefs and miles of sweeping sand beaches. This tiny land is bordered by forbidding barriers of huge, black, basalt rocks and sheer, high cliffs. From the ocean, it has the look of an impenetrable fortress, and it is easy to see how the ancient story of Uoke came into being. According to island legend, this supernatural strong man traveled about the Pacific with a huge lever. He liked to pry up whole islands and toss them into the ocean to disappear forever. However, when he came to the island—later called Easter—he ran into trouble. He did manage to pry up much of the coastal land. But when he reached a certain section of cliffs, his lever broke. Uoke left, defeated and angry. What remained was that part of the island which the god could not pry up and throw away.

Fishing was a hazardous business for the ancient islanders, and they did not have an easy time of it when it came to planting. Easter is a small island, fourteen miles long and seven miles at its widest. It was created by the eruption of three volcanoes. Each sits in a corner of the triangular-shaped land. In the center of the island, the swelling hillocks and stretches of plains are so riddled with lava stones they might almost be called cobbled. Furthermore, the volcanic ash which comprises the soil is so porous that rainfall quickly seeps away. There is not a single stream on all the island.

Nor is the climate the constantly sunny and smiling one ordinarily associated with Polynesia. Easter lies near the northern border of the southern Temperate Zone. The temperature is comfortable—semitropical. But strong sea winds continually make new cloud formations, and in moments, a sunny field can change to an eerie landscape of swift-moving shadows. While one area basks peaceably, a howling storm may suddenly deluge another part of the land.

It would seem that the ancient islanders might have had

enough to keep them busy merely in order to exist in this inhospitable place.

All of which makes the mysteries more intense.

Why, on this desolate and most isolated island in the world, did Stone Age men develop their unique culture?

Why did that culture die?

And why did the descendants of the remarkable statue-makers turn into the "savages" the early discoverers met when they ventured ashore? These natives had their own unique cults and customs (including cannibalism) which were described by the handful of Europeans who managed to reach Easter in the eighteenth and nineteenth centuries. In the twentieth century, a few scientists came to the island. Ethnologists recorded tribal life—and tribal memories. And anthropologists confirmed, by scientific means, the historic truth which lay behind the most important of the island legends. The anthropologists did more. They revealed a secret island past which even surprised the natives.

Without the detailed diaries, notes, drawings, and the anthropological digs made by this handful of outsiders— sailors, priests, and scientists—we would have no way of knowing where fantasy ended and truth began in the maze of memories and legends passed on by generations of islanders.

These discoverers play an integral role in revealing the story of Easter Island.

chapter 2

The island now called Easter, its living population, and their towering stone ancestor-statues remained completely unknown to the outside world until the early eighteenth century. And then it was the most modern of motives—the competition of businessmen—which caused the island to be discovered.

In the year 1721, the Dutch West India Company was running a slow second to the Dutch East India Company, which had taken over wealthy trading posts in the Dutch East Indies and in Japan.

The directors of the Dutch West India Company decided they would have to try harder, and one day, one of them came to a meeting carrying a publication on the South Seas. It contained a description of a discovery by a British sea captain named Edward Davis, who was reputed to be something of a pirate. In any case, he was nothing of an explorer. In the year 1687, he had, according to his journal, sighted in the South Pacific: "a sandy beach, with high mountains behind it." He estimated that the land lay "500 leagues due east of Capayapo."

Instead of investigating further to see whether he had perhaps rivaled Columbus by discovering a new continent, the unenterprising Captain Davis promptly turned tail and sailed toward Peru.

Nevertheless, because of his logbook entries, the mysterious land he had sighted was written about with some speculation. It became known as "Davis Land," and during the years which followed, numerous navigators set out to see if they could find the place. No one could. Some decided it had been a seascape mirage. But others remained certain that Davis had sighted a new "Southern continent."

Then a new theory arose: that the Southern continent had sunk, and the mountaintops spotted by Davis were all that remained above the water. But what glories of gold and silver, what splendors of the lost civilization there might be just below the sea!

On the tenth of April, 1721, the determined directors of the Dutch West India Company firmly resolved to send out a special expedition with strict orders to discover Davis Land come hell—or high water. This discovery, they fervently hoped, would put *their* company far ahead of the Dutch East India Company, whose coffers were overflowing with guilders and gold.

The company hired a Dutch sea captain, Jacob Roggoveen, as commander in chief of the expedition. They outfitted three sailing ships, the largest of which was the *Arend*—forty yards long. It was "mounted with thirty-two pieces of Cannon, manned with 110 Persons." And each of the three ships was "victualled for twenty-eight months."[1]

By the following April, and long before the "victuals" had run out, the three ships had come, as Roggoveen noted in his log:

> . . . about 500 miles to the Westward of Copayapo, situated on the Coast of Chile . . . and not yet come in sight of the unknown Southland [according to existing accounts of it], for the discovery of which our Expedition is specially undertaken.

In fact, the Captain had come a good bit farther than "500 miles westward of Copayapo." Indeed, he had come farther than the 500 leagues (1,500 miles) mentioned in Captain Davis' logbook. Roggoveen's ships had traveled 2,200 miles from the coast of Chile. The Dutchman wrote his discouraged notation at noon on Thursday, the second of April, 1722. It was, incidentally, Easter Day.

That same afternoon something was sighted. A turtle. And somewhat later—land! Roggoveen wrote:

> A low and flattish island lying away to starboard. . . . There was great rejoicing and everyone hoped that this low land might prove to be a foretoken of the coastline of the unknown Southern continent.

This "low and flattish island" was obviously not the mountainous land Davis had sighted.

The place appeared on no map. Therefore, it needed a name. Since it was Easter Day, Roggoveen dubbed the newly discovered island *Paasch Eyland* (Easter Island).

Darkness was falling swiftly, so it was decided to wait until dawn before proceeding further in order to determine whether they had merely stumbled on a single empty island or—as they all fervently hoped—an island which was, in fact, "a foretoken" of an entire and unknown Southern continent.

At dawn, part of the answer became clear. As the ships drew closer to the land, the seamen saw smoke.

The place was populated!

But was it safe to venture ashore?

Commander in chief Roggoveen met with the captain of each of the three ships, and they decided to:

> . . . send close in to the land two well manned shallops, properly armed (that we may be in state of defence in case

of any hostile meeting), and show all friendliness towards the inhabitants. . . . It is farther decided that both the shallops of the Ships *Arend* and *Thienhoven* shall proceed at daybreak, and that *The African Galley* should follow as close to the land as possible and prudent, covering and defending the said shallops (should need arise).[2]

But a storm arose, with thunder, sheet lightning, and showers, and the trip to shore had to be delayed.

On Monday April 6, Cornelis Bowman, Captain of the *Thienhoven,* looked overboard and saw a native who had ventured out in his one-man reed canoe. They brought him on board—the first Easter Islander ever to be viewed by the civilized world. He was, Roggoveen noted primly, "quite nude, without the slightest covering for that which modesty shrinks from revealing."

The islander proved to be a cheerful and inquisitive chap. He ran all over the ship admiring the rigging, the sails, the guns, which he "felt all over with minute attention." But what amazed him most of all was a mirror. He looked at his reflected face, "started suddenly back and then looked towards the back of the glass, apparently in the expectation of discovering there the cause of the apparition."[3]

Finally, after the Dutchmen had "sufficiently beguiled ourselves with him, and he with us," they sent him back to the island in his canoe. But they sent him back richer than he had come. They gave him a mirror, a pair of scissors, and "other like trifles," which included two strings of blue glass beads which he wore round his neck.

The adventurous islander evidently inspired others to pay their respects to the strangers, for the following day when the ships had anchored a quarter mile off the coast, a whole slew of canoes came tipping through the stormy waves. Another contingent of natives swam from shore. And the three ships were soon overrun with excited islanders.

They showed, Roggoveen wrote, "their great cupidity for everything they saw; and were so daring that they took the seamen's hats and caps from their heads, and sprang overboard with their spoil." One enterprising fellow climbed in through the window from his canoe and made off with a tablecloth. "One must take special heed," Roggoveen wrote with irritation, "to keep close watch over everything."

The commander and one of his crewmates, Carl Friederich Behrens, noted several surprising facts about the islanders who swarmed over the ships.

Some wore large white chocks of wood in their artificially extended shoulder-length ear lobes. And many who sported the dangling lobes also had shaven heads.

There were men dressed only in tattoos of "wonderful birds and animals" which covered the body so completely that no skin color could be seen. Many of those whose skin did show had the golden brown skin color and flat-nosed look of Polynesians. They had dark eyes, black hair and, like other South Sea islanders, they were beardless. But there were some who had greenish eyes, pale skins, red hair, and long beards. "One," wrote Roggoveen, "was an entirely white man who was wearing white chocks of wood in his ears as large as fists."

But what startled the Dutchmen most was the sight they beheld the next morning as they stood on deck studying the island. Gigantic statues were stationed all along the coast. They stood singly or in a line, on high altars.

The islanders had kindled hundreds of fires before the stone giants, and they squatted in the shadow of the statues, soles of their feet flat against the ground, heads bent in reverence. Then, with the palms of their hands pressed together, they raised and lowered their arms until, as the sun rose, they lay prostrate before the monoliths.

Later that morning, 134 Dutchmen ventured ashore, each armed with musket, pistols and cutlass. Because of the rearing boulders, they anchored their shallops offshore, and then clambered over the rocks—slipping, sliding, yet trying to proceed in dignified "open order."

Once on land, they marched forward rather nervously, signaling the curious hordes of natives to "stand out of our way and make room for us."

Suddenly, to everyone's astonishment, four or five shots rang out from the rear, followed by a shout. " 'T is tyd, 't is tyd, geeft vuur!" ("It's time, it's time, fire!") Whereupon more than thirty shots were fired. The islanders raced off in panic. But some remained behind: the ten or twelve who had been killed, and the many more who lay wounded.

An immediate order went out in Dutch. No more firing!

And then came the question: Who had started the shooting? And why?

Finally, a shamefaced assistant pilot came up to Roggoveen and confessed that one of the natives had grabbed at his gun. Whereupon, the pilot struck the fellow a blow. Meanwhile, another native had tried to strip the jacket off a seaman— who resisted. Seeing all this, other islanders picked up stones and used threatening gestures, "as if to pelt us with them." said the pilot in fainthearted explanation. "Whereby, from all appearance, the firing on the part of my small troop was brought about."[4]

Despite this disastrous start, Roggoveen managed, by sign language, to get a complicated message across to those natives who were brave enough—or curious enough—to show their faces once more. He explained that the victims had "threatened to make assault upon us by stone-throwing," and he assured the islanders there would be no more shooting.

They evidently believed him for they soon brought an array of sugar cane, fowl, yams, and bananas which they spread before the seamen. "We gave them to understand," wrote Roggoveen, "that we desired nothing excepting only sixty fowls and thirty bunches of bananas, for which we paid them ample in striped linen."

However, some of the younger women must have surmised that the seamen desired something more than bananas. Unlike the men on the island, the women were clothed. Each wore a wrap and a hat made of rushes. "They sat down before us," wrote Behrens, "and disrobed."

Roggoveen and Behrens made copious notes on all aspects of island life. Then on Friday, April 10, the Dutchmen sailed off in search of the Southern continent, steering west and expressing the hope, as the commander in chief put it: "that a good discovery of a high and wide-stretching tract of land should result after a little while."

They did not discover the Southern continent. Nor did Roggoveen feel he had made any contribution by the island he *did* discover. But his diary and that of his shipmate Behrens —containing page after page of detailed description of the prehistoric people of Easter Island—have proved more valuable than any gold or precious metals, which the directors of the Dutch West India Company had hoped he would find. (The Directors may not have agreed with this. But future generations of scholars, travelers, and Easter Island enthusiasts certainly do.)

A half century later, the Spanish government decided to take over the island discovered—but never claimed by—the Dutch. The place would not exactly be a pearl in the crown of King Carlos III, but it was hoped that an expedition would also discover that illusive Southern continent sighted so long ago by Captain Davis, which would make an impressive addition to the fast-disappearing Spanish Empire.

Don Felipe Gonzalez de Haedo was put in charge of the

two-ship expedition which sailed from Peru on October 10, 1770. Within five weeks, they had reached Easter.

They spent the entire first day "in quest of a harbor."

The second day, they encircled the island by launch, making an excellent map of the coastline and "giving names to the points, bays &c." By nightfall, they had bestowed a whole assortment of Spanish names: there was the Cape of San Antonio, the Cape of San Christoval, the Cape of San Francisco, the headland of San Felipe, and a cove called Langara, named after a senior lieutenant on board. All this before they had so much as set foot on the newly named San Carlos Island.

Finally, on the afternoon of the following day, they beached a launch near "Cape San Francisco" where they were promptly surrounded by naked natives who offered fruits and hens. Langara issued orders that no one, "under pain of a severe flogging should accept any article from the islanders without giving some equivalent in return."

This proved a wise order. The islanders seemed pleased with their friendly visitors, so much so that some 800 of them followed the Spaniards with high enthusiasm as the visitors carried three heavy crosses to the top of a three-humped hill on a peninsula the natives called Poike. As they ran along, the islanders kept crying, "Maca Maca," which—the Spaniards soon discovered—was the name of the chief god of Easter Island. Spanish sailors, under the direction of two Spanish priests, set up a cross on each of the hill humps. Then the chaplains chanted litanies, and the natives joined in the Latin responses: *ora pro nobis.* The Spaniards fired three volleys of musketry; the ships replied with twenty-one gun salutes. And the island was officially declared to be Spanish territory.

To make the proceedings still more legal, a few natives— those who had not been scared off by the gunfire—were encouraged to sign the document which had been prepared in advance by the Most Excellent Señor the Viceroy, Governor, and Captain-General of the Kingdom of Peru. The natives obliged by making the following signs at the foot of the paper.

What the signs meant no one knew. But the Spaniards declared that the signatures made the document legal. The island aborigines were now official subjects of the King of Spain.

Then, according to Don Felipe's diary, the King's new subjects joined in "the joyful shout of *Viva el Rey*." (Long live the King.) "The islanders responded with our own people; they pronounce with such ease that they repeat whatever is said to them, just like ourselves."

According to the detailed journals kept by Don Felipe and his two pilots, the Spanish seamen were impressed with these new subjects. Not only could they repeat words in Latin and French, but, wrote Hervé, one of the pilots, "if they wore clothing like ourselves they might very well pass for Europeans." Many of the men were "thickly bearded, tall, well set up, white and ruddy." Others were "swarthy or reddish skinned, but not thick lipped nor flat nosed." As to their hair coloring: "some have it black, some chestnut colored and limp, and others tending to red or cinnamon tint."

They looked nothing like South American Indians. Most

of them were lighter-skinned than natives on other South Sea islands.

Where had these people come from? How had they managed to cross many hundreds of miles of empty ocean? How had they found this tiny speck of an island which sat between the vastness of sea and sky?

The most amazing mystery of all was the statues. One of the pilots, Agüera, hit a statue with a hoe—and sparks flew out. "The material of the statue is," he concluded, "very hard stone."

After further exploration of the island, he wrote that there was nothing whatever to act as a lever for raising the statues, or for getting the massive topknots onto their heads. "Not a single tree is to be found capable of furnishing a plank so much as six inches in width." Agüera concluded: "That a people lacking machinery and the materials for constructing any should be able to raise . . . a statue of such height causes wonder. . . . Much remains to be worked out on this subject."

After six days, the Spaniards sailed away.

Despite the fact that they were so impressed with the natives, and with the stone colossi which girded the coast, the Spaniards made no further attempt to return to San Carlos Island. The fact that the place had been claimed for the king of Spain made no difference to anyone, ever.

The islanders, of course, had no idea that their domain had been legally renamed San Carlos. Nor did they know that other men called it Easter.

They had their own names for their land.

The oldest of the names, that which lived on through the island legends, was *Te Pito o te Henua*. It was a strange name for a people who were perhaps the most isolated on earth. It was a name which showed that they felt themselves to be at the very center of things. It meant: "The Navel of the World."

chapter 3

Four years after the Spaniards sailed out, the British sailed into Easter's history.

Captain James Cook had won much fame and some fortune by an exploratory trip around the world on which he made the first reliable map locating many Pacific islands. Now, on his second voyage to the South Seas, Captain Cook and his crew (which included two naturalists) came to Easter.

They arrived in desperate need of fresh water and food, and found little of anything.

The natives brought them a plentiful supply of water. But it turned out to be salty. Astonished, Cook observed that some of the islanders "drank plentifully of it; so far will necessity and custom get the better of nature!"

Finally, toward the eastern end of the island, the thirsty Englishmen found a well

> . . . whose water was perfectly fresh, but it was dirty, owing to the filthiness or uncleanness (call it what you will) of the natives, who never go to drink without washing themselves all over as soon as they have done; and if ever so many of them are together, the one leaps right in the middle of the hole, drinks, and washes himself without the least ceremony; after which another takes his place and does the same.[1]

As for fresh food supplies, Cook and his men were offered a few scrawny fowls. But rats were regarded by the islanders as too rare and tasty a treat to part with. The few vegetables that the natives planted—"yams, sweet potatoes, taraoreddy-root, plantains, sugar-canes"—were in such short supply that there was very little to spare "to supply the wants of strangers."

The only product which seemed to be in plentiful supply was sweet potatoes. And the British bought many baskets of them—only to find that the natives had filled the baskets with stones, placing a covering layer of sweet potatoes on top.

Aside from the few fowls and rats, Cook saw no animals on the island at all—edible or otherwise, "nor indeed anything which can induce ships that are not in the utmost distress, to touch at this island."

Cook also complained about the pilfering, which seemed to have reached a new level. "It was . . . hardly possible to keep anything in our pockets, nor even what themselves had sold us; for they would watch every opportunity to snatch it from us, so that we sometimes bought the same thing two or three times over, and after all did not get it."

Wars must have raged on the island during the four years which had passed since the Spanish visit. Not only had the population shrunk from several thousand to 600 or 700 (though Cook realized that many more may have been hiding in caves), but the people themselves seemed to have shrunk. They were no longer the tall, handsome savages described in impressive terms by the Spaniards. They were now small, skinny, miserable-looking men. (Most of the women kept out of sight—except for those who distributed their favors to the sailors "in the shadows cast by the giant statues.")

Even some of the statues were in a sad state.

Cook, and the two naturalists, Forster and his son, were the first to report that some of the statues had been shoved from their altars, and broken by the fall. Reporting on what they found on the east coast, near the sea, Cook wrote, "We met with three platforms of stone-work or rather the ruins of them. On each had stood four of those large statues, but they were all fallen down from two of them, and also one from the third; all except one were broken by the fall, or in some measure defaced."

Most of the statues were, however, still standing, staring out over the island, each with the same strange supercilious look of a superman who knows mysteries that mere humans can never fathom.

Captain Cook, like those who had come before, and those who were to come after, was awed and baffled by the stone giants. "It was incomprehensible to me how such great masses could be formed by a set of people among whom we saw no tools. We could hardly conceive how these islanders, wholly unacquainted with any mechanical powers, could raise such stupendous figures, and afterwards place the large cylindric stones upon their heads."

Another architectural feature baffled and awed the Englishmen: the huge altars on which the statues stood. *Ahus,* the natives called them. Cook wrote: "They are faced with hewn stones of very large size; and the workmanship is not inferior to the best plain piece of masonry we have in England. They use no cement, yet the joints are exceedingly close, and the stones morticed and tenanted one into another, in a very artful manner."

On board Cook's ship, there was a Tahitian who understood some of the words spoken by the Easter Islanders. Theirs was, he said, a Polynesian dialect related to his own Tahitian tongue.

He informed the captain that the monumental statues were not regarded as gods, but rather as memorials of dead kings.

The natives had given names to many of the statues, and some of the names were prefixed by the title *Ariki,* meaning king or chief.

Human bones strewn on top of the ahus and stuck in between the stones showed that they had been and still were being used as burial places.

After five days, which included two extensive exploratory shore visits, the British sailed away. Captain Cook summed up his impressions by writing: "No nation need contend for the honour of the discovery of this island. . . . Here is no safe anchorage, no wood for fuel, nor any fresh water worth taking on board. Nature has been exceedingly sparing of her favours to this spot."

Yet, despite Captain Cook's many caustic comments about the island, it was his published story—including vivid descriptions of the colossal statues—which brought Easter Island the international fame it has known ever since.

A Long Eared islander. Adapted from a drawing made by a member of Captain Cook's crew in 1770.

Twelve years after the British captain sailed away, a French nobleman, Jean-François de Galaup, Comte de la Pérouse, landed on the island, drawn there by the only aspect of Easter which had awed and impressed Captain Cook: the "stupendous figures of stone."

Unlike Cook, who had come to the island with a miserable crew of men sick with scurvy, half-starved and desperate for fresh drinking water— the Comte de la Pérouse arrived with a healthy and well-provisioned crew. Furthermore, the French count came like a minor Noah. He brought to the island a pair of hogs, a pair of goats, and three sheep. In addition, he brought a gardener, who went about the island sowing cabbage, carrots, beets, maize, pumpkins, and a variety of fruit trees as well as cottonseeds. He did his best to show the natives how to plant and cultivate. But his best was not good enough, for not one of the La Pérouse plants or animals were ever seen by future visitors to the island.

The Frenchman also came with artists who made accurate studies of the ancient statues, altars, boat-shaped houses, and all other remnants of ancient architecture. They later made engravings to decorate the count's published narrative of his round-the-world trip. One of these illustrated a notable trait of the islanders which was commented upon by all who visited Easter. A crew member was distracted by a topless girl, as an islander picked his pocket. Another native in the shadow of a statue, slyly filched a tricornered hat.

The count took a rough count of the islanders and estimated the population to be at least 2,000, with men, women and children in normal proportions. The volcanic island had hundreds of large natural caves and underground caverns, and it became clear that the better—and better-looking—part of the population had hidden from the Englishmen.

Perhaps, La Pérouse suggested, all this friendliness for the

French came from the fact that Captain Cook and his sailors had treated the natives well; consequently, they lost fear of visitors. Or, perhaps it was that the natives no longer feared themselves. The tribal wars which had apparently wracked the island between the Spanish and British visits were now, quite obviously, over. Harmony and good cheer seemed the prevailing mood among the populace.

The surgeon-major of the expedition described the islanders in glowing terms: "Instead of meeting with men exhausted by famine . . . I found, on the contrary, a considerable population, with more beauty and grace than I afterwards met with in any other island."

Yet, despite all this apparent happiness, the natives of Easter inexplicably kept on destroying the statues—the one feature of their island which made them unique in all the world. In 1804, a Russian, Lisjanskij, circumnavigated the island and counted only twenty statues still standing on their ahus. In 1816, another Russian, Kotzebue, reported that most of the statues described by his countryman as still being up, now were down.

In 1838, Admiral du Petit-Thouars sailed around the island, and saw only two ahus on which statues still stood; four on one, five on the others. He was the last person from the outside world to see Easter Island statues standing where they had been set up by the prehistoric Stone Age men who made them.

But whatever misfortune the islanders may have inflicted upon their monuments—and upon themselves—it was the outside world which very nearly brought an end to all human life on Easter Island.

In December 1862, eight Peruvian slave ships descended on the island.

The slave market in the United States had dried up, since

the states were embroiled in a Civil War. But a new slave market had opened in South America. It had been found that guano—a substance formed by the droppings of sea birds— could profitably be sold as fertilizer. The problem was that workers would not go voluntarily to the "guano islands" off the coast of Peru. The tiny islets were baking hot, barren, miserable places. The solution: slavery.

Two weeks prior to Christmas Day, eighty armed men went ashore at Easter and they spread enticing gifts on the ground. But these were not Christmas presents. As the excited natives examined the gifts, the Peruvian slave raiders attacked. Shots split the air. Twelve islanders were killed. Others escaped by scrambling up the rocks or diving into the sea. But over 200 were thrown to the ground, tied up, and transported to the waiting ships. There they encountered hundreds more who had been captured earlier when they came out to trade with the seamen.

The eight ships sailed off with a cargo of over 1,000 islanders chained in the hold. Among them was the island king, Kai Makoi, and six of his sons and daughters.

The human cargo was sold to the guano companies in Peru, and sent at once to the offshore islands. There they swiftly began to die, killed by disease and the intolerable conditions under which they were forced to work.

Finally, the Bishop of Tahiti learned of the matter, and he became so enraged that he protested to the French Minister in Peru. The Minister, in turn, protested to the Peruvian authorities—and they ordered that the enslaved islanders be sent back to Easter.

But by the time ships arrived to take them home, 900 had died. Of the one hundred who still survived, many were sick with smallpox. When the vessels reached Easter, all but fifteen islanders had perished.

Upon seeing the ships, the residents of Easter hid in caves, terrified of further slave raids.

The islanders could not, however, hide from the disease germs the returnees had brought with them. A smallpox epidemic raged and killed off most of the remaining population.

The following year, the first outsider in Easter's history came to live on the island.

La Pérouse and his men had stayed only ten hours, though they made extensive expeditions and notes during that time. Captain Cook and his men had spent two days ashore. The Spaniards were offshore for almost a week, but spent only a few days on Easter. And the island's discoverer, Roggoveen, remained on the island only a day.

The few others who had tried to land during the years were prevented from doing so by wild waves and a rocky coastline, or by the natives who pelted them with a storm of stones.

But Brother Eugène Eyraud was determined to live on the island, and to convert every last native to Christianity.

Eyraud had come as a very young man from France to South America where he felt prospects were better for earning money. It was not for himself he needed the money, but for his brother who was studying to become a priest and a missionary.

Eyraud was working as a mechanic in Chile when he met, quite by chance, two French priests. They informed him that he himself could become a missionary, without even being a priest.

As a novice with the Fathers of the Holy Spirit, lay Brother Eugène left Chile with other missionaries: their destination and destiny, Easter Island. Or so they all thought when departing from Chile.

Their first stop, however, was Tahiti—a strange detour,

since Tahiti is twice as far from Chile as is Easter Island. The year was 1862—the same year that the slave ships descended upon Easter. When the missionaries got word of this, they decided to abandon their plans to go to Easter. What use to bring Christianity to the remnant of a population which had been left on this isolated island?

But Brother Eugène was, perhaps, more dedicated than the priests. In any case, he insisted that he would settle alone on Easter and prepare the way for the full-fledged priests who would, hopefully, follow.

On the second day of the new year, 1864, a schooner anchored off Cook's Bay, known by the natives as Hanga-roa. The passenger list included Brother Eugène Eyraud; an Easter Islander named Pana who had been taken off to Peru by the slave traders, but escaped and made his way to Tahiti; and a man named Daniel from the Polynesian island Mangareva.

Daniel was sent ashore to investigate the situation on Easter. He returned, terrorized, and told Brother Eugène that he had been met by a hoard of demons painted black and red who leaped into the air, shouting, shrieking, and waving spears. "I would not go ashore again for a thousand piastres," he exclaimed. "They are horrible-looking people. . . . They are threatening . . . and smallpox is ravaging the island. You cannot possibly land."[2]

Everyone on the ship insisted on returning to Tahiti at once —with the exception of Brother Eugène and Pana.

The captain agreed to send the two men ashore in a longboat while the schooner remained anchored in Hanga-roa Bay. This was the place which had been chosen as a landing site by all the visitors who had thus far arrived on the island. However, none of the other visitors had arrived with luggage. The captain informed the brother that it would be too risky to try landing anything other than men at Hanga-roa. At least if rough waves tipped over the longboat, men could swim for it. And men could, if necessary, clamber over the rocks jutting out near the shore.

Pana seconded the idea of landing at Hanga-roa since, he said, many of his brethren lived around this bay at the western end of the island. It was, therefore, decided that the two men would go without luggage. If they got safely ashore, then the captain would sail his schooner to the northeast coast and land Brother Eugène's belongings at one of the island's two small sand beaches, Anakena.

Since Pana had but few belongings, he took them with him in the longboat. However, no sooner had they made it to shore, than everything Pana owned was stolen by the waiting crowd. Seeing this, Brother Eugène was anxious to leave at once for Anakena. He did not want all his things stolen if the ship arrived at the beach before he did. However, every time he and Pana tried to depart, they were dragged back and surrounded again by natives who looked far from friendly.

Eugène later wrote:

> Daniel must certainly be pardoned for getting afraid. A multitude of men, women and children that could amount to about twelve hundred, had nothing reassuring about them. The men were armed with a kind of lance formed by a stick at the end of which was fixed a sharp stone. These savages are tall, strong and well built. Most of them are naked. The feathers they wear as ornaments, their tattoos, their savage cries, give altogether a dreadful appearance.

Finally, Pana persuaded some warriors to act as a protection service for the long trek through the tall grass and rocky lava fields.

They finally reached Anakena which the brother regarded as a heavenly haven. And, indeed, it looked the part. The beach—small, broad, with pinkish sand—was protected by outstretched arms of land. The sand sloped gently into the water, making the spot ideal for swimming. It was not, however—as Pana well knew—ideal for landing. Out past the cape, there were often unexpectedly big breakers which could fling a small landing craft straight into the air.

In any case, Brother Eugène spent a pleasant evening under the warm summer skies in company of Pana, the escort of warriors—who had by now become quite friendly—and several massive statues which lay face down where they seemed to be sleeping through the centuries. There was something else which pleased him about Anakena. Pana had learned some French while in Tahiti, and was able to tell his fascinated audience of one tales about the island's first King, the great Hotu Matua, who had come from a far-off place called Hiva and had chosen to land on this very beach. Indeed, Pana showed Brother Eugène the cave in which the royal family had lived while their house was being built. The cave was named *ana kena* (cave of the kena bird). Though natives now called the whole beach area Anakena, many still referred to it as the King's Beach, or the Valley of the Kings. Pana also pointed out the stone foundations of the great king's beachfront dwelling.

The next morning Brother Eugène was up at dawn and, much to his relief, saw the schooner. He stood on the beach ready to welcome his belongings. These included carpenter's tools, wooden planks for building his home and church, a church bell, five sheep, a bag of flour, clothing, cuttings of trees, and a Tahitian catechism.

Then, as he watched in horror, he saw the ship held back by roaring waves trying again and again to get closer to shore. Finally, the schooner sailed off and disappeared beyond the horizon, leaving Eugène Eyraud with nothing but the clothes he wore. What he mourned most of all however was the loss of "the Tahitian catechism with which to teach the Kanakas prayers and the fundamental truths of religion."

That evening, however, good news came. The schooner had not, after all, returned to Tahiti. The brother's belongings had been landed at Hanga-roa.

The missionary, Pana, and their escort of warriors immediately set out to rush back through the darkness, hoping to reach Hanga-roa before all of Brother Eugène's possessions were stolen.

Upon arrival, Brother Eugène was met by one native arrayed in his frockcoat; another sported the missionary's hat. Others were gathered around the planks, arguing as to what they were used for. Worn out though he was from the difficult cross-country race, Brother Eugène settled the debate by hammering the boards into place and making himself a hut—with a door replete with lock. Then he locked inside those of his possessions which had not been stolen.

Life was not easy, but at least—for a time—it did not seem to be dangerous.

The islanders were in a sad state. As though the smallpox epidemic had not wreaked enough havoc, the survivors had fought each other for possession of the rocky fields left by the dead. There had been so much fighting that there was little time for planting, and famine had spread its skeleton hands over the land.

Brother Eugène found a people who cared nothing about its past—or present. They did, however, believe in an afterlife where a good man would live in a fine dwelling with a plentiful supply of food and passionate women. Some good men were so anxious to reach this privileged state that they committed suicide by jumping off the cliffs. The souls of those who had been bad had to hang about near their corpses. The more evil they had been on earth, the more hungry and thirsty were they in death. (Often a kind living relative took pity and left food for them in or on the grave.)

Chief of the many island gods was *Ko Make-Make* who decided, among other things, what fate would be meted out to each islander who died. Make-Make's anger could be heard whenever thunder sounded in the skies.

When Brother Eugène started to teach *his* religion, many islanders came to listen, mainly because they had nothing much else to do. He was the chief source of entertainment on Easter. He provoked much laughter, debate, and comment. If he retired to his hut and they wanted him to perform, they would "knock all round the house. Then they sit down a little way off and throw stones, first little ones, then bigger ones to keep the game interesting. . . . I am the stranger, the *papa,* whom everyone wants to know, to see working, and above all, to exploit."

But there were rewards.

After some months, a few of the islanders were able to read, still more could spell, and quite a number—including children —had learned to chant Latin prayers.

In addition, Brother Eugène discovered a remarkable remnant of the ancient statue builders; something which had never before been seen by an outsider: the *rongorongo* boards.

He wrote:

> In all their houses one can find tablets of wood or sticks covered with many kinds of hieroglyphic signs . . . which the natives trace by means of sharp stones. . . . Each figure has its own name, but the little they make of these tablets makes me inclined to think that these signs, the rest of a primitive script, are for them at present a custom which they preserve without searching the meaning.

Although the natives could write the hieroglyphics, there was not a single person on the island who could read them.

Then, as he learned to speak to the islanders in their own language, he learned the true tragedy of the rongorongo boards. The full name of the tablets was *ko hau motu mo rongorongo,* which meant "lines of script for recitation." According to island legend, Chief Hotu Matua had brought with him sixty-seven of these tablets. And he had also brought men who knew the art of writing and reading them. These masters *(maori ko hau rongorongo)* had passed their knowledge down through the generations of islanders. But all of the remaining maori ko hau rongorongo had been captured by the slave traders, and had died.

If Brother Eugène Eyraud had arrived on Easter only thirteen months earlier—before the arrival of the slave ships—he would undoubtedly have learned the secrets of reading the rongorongo tablets, and many of the mysteries concerning the prehistoric statue builders might have been resolved.

In September, after he had been on the island almost nine months, the yearly festival of the birdman took place: "the time of *Mataveri.*" Brother Eugène later described it as "a sort of country-gathering where everybody reunites for a period of two months, with foot races and all possible pass-time exercises. The natives all put on their best attire and paint their faces and bodies in the most artistic manners; long-eared women putting enormous bark-rolls into the apertures of the lobes." (At this point in time, only the women of Easter lengthened their lobes.)

But the Mataveri period was more than mere fun and games. At the end of the two months, "the pillages and incendiary fires commence."

Brother Eugène had acquired a protector named Torometi. In fact, the missionary longed to be protected from his protector, for—as he put it—"this rum customer continued, with great persistence, to relieve me on every possible occasion of everything I had brought with me, although it was not bothering me at all."

As the time of Mataveri approached, Torometi told the missionary that everything Brother Eugène (still) owned would have to be hidden away in a cave. Otherwise, it would be stolen by others during the festival time.

The brother refused. Whereupon, Torometi, his wife, and several neighbors "caught hold of me and made all resistance impossible. They took possession of my keys, carried away the property they found, and left me with hardly anything but my mattress and locked-up tool boxes. When this operation was terminated they gave me the keys back."

In an effort to escape from his protector, Brother Eugène fled. But Torometi and his followers found him, seized him by the arms and legs and dragged him along the stony ground until the brother, bruised and bleeding, promised to follow Torometi around like a slave.

This he did. But one day during the festival proceedings, another band of warriors burned Torometi's hut, and took his "slave" as their prize. They stole his coat, shoes, and trousers, and left him as naked as they were. Then they knocked him cold with a well-aimed stone.

That night, the missionary made his way back to his hut where he managed to find an old pair of shoes and a blanket. He then fled to Vai-hu, over three miles away, where he lived in a cave—and continued to give daily lessons to natives who had followed him there.

Eight days later, he heard the shout, *"Pahi! Pahi!"* A boat! A schooner anchored in Hanga-roa Bay.

Clad in his blanket, Brother Eugène went down to the shore with a horde of natives who were so excited by the sight of the ship that they forgot their warfare. They danced about, shrieked, and yelled. And Torometi put Brother Eugène on his shoulders and carried him out to the whaleboat which had been lowered from the ship and was close to shore. The sailors, terrified by the screaming, jumping, dancing natives, grabbed the white man and rowed back to the schooner as fast as they could. On board, the shaggy-bearded, near-naked brother, met two priests from Chile who had come out to find whether he was alive or dead.

After describing his most recent adventures, Brother Eugène asked to be returned to the island. The horrified captain refused, and with the good brother aboard, promptly set sail for Chile.

The following year some Peruvian sailors visited Easter, and never left. They were eaten.

Then in March 1866, the brave Brother Eugène returned. He had persuaded a priest, Père Hippolyte Roussel, to join him. Later that year, two more priests arrived. A small church was built in Hanga-roa, another in Vai-hu. The fathers and Brother Eugène lived in a corrugated iron hut, which they had brought along. The hut could be locked securely, and could not be burned down. It could also be used by the islanders as a giant drum. Wrote Brother Eugène, "The whole multitude of grown-up children immediately surrounded the cabin, dancing, shouting, drumming on the metal sheets, and every now and then sending a hail of stones rattling onto the roof."

Despite the constant pranks played on them by the natives, the priests felt they were making progress. The two churches were filled on Sundays. And most of the islanders had been baptized.

The strongest holdouts were the chiefs who did not take to the idea of giving up their many wives. This particular provision of Christianity had not concerned the other natives, since few of them could afford more than one wife in any case.

Finally, however, the chiefs agreed to become monogamous. At least, they showed up in church on Sundays with only one wife in tow.

In August 1868, Brother Eugène died. His last words were: "Are they all baptized?"

"All," he was told.

He was the first European to live and to die on Easter Island.

chapter 4

T wo years after the passing of Brother Eugène, another Frenchman arrived on the island—an opposite in character of the good brother.

Captain Dutroux-Bornier was master of the schooner which had brought the last two missionaries to Easter Island. In 1866, he wrote to them, commending them for the fine work they had done on the island. He predicted a great future for Easter. And in 1870 he arrived, replete with sheep and supplies, to help bring that future into being—with himself as the beneficiary rather than the benefactor.

He paid some natives with pieces of cloth and thereby purchased a large tract of land at Mataveri. Tormeti—Brother Eugène's erstwhile protector—now became Dutroux-Bornier's protector, or more accurately, commander of a small army of bodyguards surrounding the Frenchman. Torometi soon had visions of becoming a powerful chief with "the vanquished people of Hanga-roa and Vai-hu" as his slaves.

Dutroux-Bornier was not averse to this slave idea. Raids were made on Hanga-roa. Huts were burned. People were killed. After a bullet had ripped past Father Roussel's ear, the missionaries sent a complaint to the Bishop of Tahiti—who ordered that the priest and his flock should be evacuated from Easter Island.

In 1871, a ship arrived and took the priest and most of the natives to Tahiti and to Mangareva.

Six years later, Dutroux-Bornier was murdered on Easter Island. His business partner, a Mr. Brander—based in Tahiti—came to take over the sheep farm, bringing with him a half-caste named Alexander Salmon as manager.

There were not many natives to manage; the population had dwindled to 111. Consequently, Salmon imported some Tahitians to help run the sheep farm—which by now had taken over most of the island. Tahitian words infiltrated into the ancient language of Easter Island.

The Tahitians renamed Easter, Rapa Nui or Great Rapa—after another Polynesian island: Rapa. That name seemed to appeal to the natives of Easter for they gave up the old name Te Pito-o-te-henua (The Navel of the World), and henceforth referred to their land as Rapa Nui—the name they still call it today.

The new manager, Alexander Salmon, was the first outsider to become fluent in the local language of the native islanders. He also knew French—and later could act as interpreter for the few Europeans who came to the island during the remainder of the nineteenth century.

Despite the fact that Salmon was related to the Tahitian royal family on his mother's side, and despite the fact that he could easily have installed himself as king or master of Easter Island—with a host of loyal Tahitians to back him—he proved to be a fine manager. He did what he could for the islanders, was kind to them, and they responded with loyalty. For a time, peace reigned once again on Easter.

In the meantime, several ships had arrived at the island. One, a Chilean corvette called *O'Higgens,* had a young cadet aboard. His name was Policarpo Toro Hurtado. Though no one suspected it at the time, he was one day to have more influence on the fate of Easter than anyone who had ever visited there before. The O'Higgens anchored in Hanga-roa Bay for eight days in 1870. This gave young Policarpo ample time to explore the island.

Although the natives had all been baptized and came to church on Sunday, most of them still went about wearing only their tattoos and as the captain of the O'Higgens noted, they were still "primitive in behavior, dancing nude in public places and performing improper and immoral movements."

As for the population in stone, not a single statue remained standing on its ahu. All had been thrown down—and many were mutilated.

Two years later a French warship, *La Flore,* anchored off Easter for five days. On board this vessel was a young midshipman who could both draw and write. His account of the island, published many years later—with his remarkably accurate drawings of the huge stone heads at Rana Raraku—once again brought Easter Island to world attention, for the midshipman had become the famed French writer, Pierre Loti. That, however, was a *nom de plume.* When he visited the island he was still known—or unknown—as Louis Viaud.

The young Frenchman got on well with the islanders. When he left, he wrote: "Really a little friendship had come up among us, perhaps as much from our deep differences as from our common childishness."

But upon his arrival, the populace did not seem all that friendly.

He came to the island in a whaleboat at five in the morning of January 4, 1872.

The sky is cold and gloomy. The trade wind throws salt spume in our faces. The island has put on its most fantastic appearance to receive us. Against the dark grays of the sky the rocks and craters seem a pale copper color. Not a tree anywhere: desert, desolation.

. . . In an instant the beach is covered with savages. They come out of every hole from cracks in the rock where they sleep, from huts so low they seem too small to harbor human beings . . . We had hardly disembarked before we were hemmed in by the men of the village. They shake in our faces in the early morning dusk their lances pointed with obsidian. . . . I am left alone crowded between my new hosts, faces and chests blue with tattooing, long hair, strange smiles. . . .

They have closed me in from all sides . . . Now they are singing, first humming but then singing a plaintive lugubrious chorus accompanied by a balancing of the head and legs as if they were enormous bears. . . . The rhythm of the song speeds up, the movement of heads and thighs becomes faster and faster, voices become hoarse and deep as the song in the wind and the sound of the sea rises to a savage clamor to the rhythm of the furious dance. . . .

Later that day:

On the rocks which rise above us facing the sea appears a whole different part of the population, more fearful. . . . These are heavily tattooed men, crouching ferociously with their hands joined across their knees; and women seated in statuesque poses with whitish cloaks around their shoulders. On their hair knotted behind they wear flowered crowns of reeds. Not a movement, not a manifestation. They are content to look at us from above and from a distance.

Then he goes on a cross-island trek.

In the distance near the sea we see something that looks like a European house. . . . It is the third habitation of the old time missionaries built at a place called Vaihou. In those days there was a happy tribe living on the beach, today no one. Vaihou is a desert and the little house is a ruin.[1]

Those "old-time missionaries" had, in fact, left Easter only six months before the young midshipman got there! In that short time, Christianity had also departed. The natives were as pagan as they had been before Brother Eugène set foot on the island.

Other visitors came to the island, made detailed reports, and sailed away.

There was a Frenchman named Pinart who landed, appropriately, on Easter Day, 1877.

A German named Geiseler came in 1882.

And in 1886, a young American named William J. Thomson arrived on the *U.S.S. Mohican.* He served as paymaster on the ship. During his eleven days on the island, he became an instant ethnologist, archaeologist, and anthropologist.

Like Pinart and Geiseler, he hired Alexander Salmon as his interpreter and guide. But unlike the two Europeans, the young American put in intensive days and nights of work. He knew what questions to ask and what areas to investigate, for he had read everything he could find about the island and had even made efforts to learn the Polynesian language.

He made voluminous notes about the life of the late-nineteenth-century natives, and he also managed to visit, measure, and describe 555 stone statues. All those which had once stood towering on their ahus lay like slain giants, faces in the dirt. Many had been beheaded.

Thomson's report was published by the American Museum in Washington D.C. in 1889.

Individuals throughout the world were fascinated by the mysteries of Easter. But so far as countries went, it seemed that the words of Captain Cook were all too true: "No nation need contend for the honour of the discovery of this island."

Spain seemed to have completely forgotten about its "San Carlos" island. The French had obtained certain rights—and then renounced them. An English commander named Clark visited the island in 1882 and suggested to his government that Easter become a British protectorate. The suggestion did not receive so much as a reply.

Then back came young Policarpo Toro Hurtado, who had first seen the island when he served as cadet on the Chilean corvette, the O'Higgens. It was he who decided that Easter Island should be acquired by Chile.

True, Easter was over 2,200 miles from Chile—a tremendous distance. On the other hand, Chile was the country closest to Easter Island.

True also, Easter lacked the obvious appeals of other Polynesian paradises (most of which had already been spoken for by other nations). There were no coral reefs to make placid harbors and picturesque lagoons, no palm trees, no lush vegetation, no bright tropical birds. The few scattered trees which now grew there were barely ten feet tall; the "flora" consisted chiefly of faded-looking dry grass. And there was virtually no "fauna" at all. On the other hand, despite the island's complete lack of natural attributes—including that all-essential, fresh water—the people of that island had once created the remarkable monoliths which had made the place famed throughout the world. The present-day offspring of these amazing prehistoric men might well have natural attributes which would help make the island a worthwhile possession.

Toro, now an officer on the O'Higgens, returned to the island in 1886, and deposited three Chilean families who would, he hoped, colonize the place. These families took a look around—and decided to return to the mainland on the O'Higgens.

Undaunted, Toro approached the proper Chilean authorities, who agreed that the annexation of Easter was a fine idea.

Consequently, in the year 1888, Policarpo Toro Hurtado—

now a captain—made his third trip to Easter Island and announced that the place henceforth belonged to Chile. The natives, he declared, should now be called *Pascuenses*— *Isla de Pascua* being the Spanish translation of Easter Island. The local language should be known as Pascuense. (The islanders, however, continued to call their land—and their language— Rapa Nui.)

Salmon and Brander had given up the sheep farm enterprise and returned to Tahiti. They had turned their business over to a British firm, Williamson, Balfour & Co., which specialized in Scottish sheep. Now, as the official owner of the island, Chile leased almost all the land to the British firm, retaining only a small area around Hanga-roa for the Pascuenses, who were told they should cultivate their own fields in this section.

The islanders seemed to have a taste for Scottish sheep,— or roast lamb—so a high fence was built to cut off the Pascuense area from the rest of the island. The natives could pass only if they had special permission.

However, so many sheep managed somehow to "pass" into the Pascuense area—without permission—that the British company put up more stone fences around the grazing lands. The builders used the most convenient large stones available —and many ancient ahus were destroyed in the effort to keep the sheep from disappearing. Nonetheless, some 3,000 continued to vanish each year. The Pascuenses insisted that the sheep were stupid: They all fell off the cliffs and drowned.

Aside from collecting a substantial fee from the British company, Chile paid little attention to her new acquisition. Every two or three years, however, she sent a naval vessel to the island to bring supplies, which were sold in the shop run by Williamson, Balfour & Co. Those Pascuenses who worked for the British were paid in pesos, and therefore, for the first time, the islanders not only had such "civilization items" as matches, nails, and underpants, which they could buy—but they had the wherewithal to purchase them. Quite a change from the previous system of barter or theft of items of apparel worn by the seamen on ships which stopped at Easter on an average of once a decade.

In the early years of the twentieth century, a new type of visitor started coming to Easter Island.

In the eighteenth and nineteenth centuries, the descriptions of the island and its inhabitants had been made, in the main, by seamen.

Now the experts started to arrive.

In 1905, a professional zoologist, Alexander Agassiz, showed up on a U.S. fish commission steamer named *Albatross*.

In 1911, the Chileans sent a botanist, a meteorologist, and a seismologist.

And in 1914, there arrived the first archaeological expedition in the island's history. It was headed by Mrs. Katherine Scoresby-Routledge, a British lady who arrived with her party in her private yacht. She spent seventeen months on Easter, interviewing all of the older islanders who remembered the legends in which their people's ancient history had been passed on through the generations. She also made careful studies of the statues, though she did no real digging—other than removing silt from the buried sections of the monoliths.

Mrs. Routledge published a fascinating book for the general public called *The Mystery of Easter Island: The Story of an Expedition*. She also wrote a few articles. But before she could get to work on the large scientific volume she planned to produce about the island, she died. No one else stepped in to make use of her boxes of invaluable notes, and, unfortunately, they all were lost.

In 1917, a Swedish botanist, C. Scottsberg, showed up on

Easter and spent ten days studying local flora—what there was of it.

In 1925, the British geologist, L. J. Chubb, put in an appearance.

And in 1934 came the largest scientific expedition yet to land on the island. It was headed by the French ethnologist, Dr. Alfred Métraux, and the Belgian anthropologist, Dr. Henri Lavachery. They spent five months on the island. But, like Mrs. Scoresby-Routledge, they were so busy interviewing the natives and surveying and mapping the ancient ahus, the old paved roads, the rock carvings, and the statues, that they had no time to look below the surface. Aside from uncovering a few of the half-buried statues, they did no digging.

The following year, another sort of expert arrived. Father Sebastian Englert was a specialist on ancient languages. He had had an early start on the subject, for his father was a professor at the Museum of Ancient Languages in Augsberg, Germany.

Father Sebastian became a Capuchin monk in 1912, and left for Chile nine years later to study Amapuchie, a Chilean Indian tongue which he learned to speak flawlessly—a unique addition to his other languages: Spanish, English, French, Latin, and his mother tongue, German. (He also read in Italian and Greek.)

In 1935, Father Sebastian came to Easter, planning a six-month's stay in order to study the ancient tongue of the islanders. But by 1935 the language, Rapa Nui, had become a mixture of ancient, modern, Tahitian, and European words. In order to discover which were the truly ancient words, Father Sebastian had to study the old legends. This led him to a study of the ancient history of Easter Island. Then, completely caught up in the fascinating world of the prehistoric islanders, he traveled around the island by horseback, sleeping

Father Sebastian Englert, the beloved priest who came to Easter in 1935, planning a six-months' stay. He remained for thirty-three years.

in caves, living off the land (his diet confined chiefly to fish and sweet potatoes). He visited every statue and painted a large white number on each to aid in description and identification. And in 1944, he published a book called *The World of Hotu Matua*. Hotu Matua was the legendary hero of the ancient islanders.

Father Sebastian's interest did not stop with the ancients. He was assigned as priest to Easter Island in 1937, and he had more influence on the life of the islanders than any other outsider in Easter's history. The island became his life and his home, and he came to know more about Easter—past and present—than anyone else in the world.

Meanwhile, despite all the sheep stealing, the managers of Williamson, Balfour & Co. had managed to do very well. By 1934, there were some 40,000 sheep running over and over-running the island.

That year, the Chilean government decided that the British company had derived quite enough profit from the island. Consequently, they refused to renew the lease. Instead, they bought the buildings and the livestock from the British and announced that, henceforth, the Chilean navy would run the vast sheep farm which the island had become. They further announced that the profits would be used to better the lot of the islanders. They built a small hospital, replete with one Chilean doctor. They started a small school with one teacher —and taught Spanish as the official language of the island. They laid out a few dirt roads, planted 1,000 eucalyptus trees, and announced that the Chilean military governor would be the sole authority on the island.

Father Sebastian had, in the meantime, converted the islanders back to Christianity. His first church was a pre-fabricated storehouse, donated by a Chilean manufacturer. His sermons were a mixture of Latin, Spanish, and Pascuense —the priest had become fluent in the native language. But the hymns were sung in the style of the ancient islanders— melodic, repetitious, and strangely hypnotic songs.

The islanders no longer went about garbed only in tattoos. Most wore European clothing although some of the women preferred Tahitian-type sarongs.

The long, low, windowless reed huts disappeared in favor of frame houses built from planks brought by the Chilean supply ship, or wood resurrected from shipwrecks.

In one generation, the islanders stepped from the Stone Age into civilization. But many Pascuenses wondered whether this had, in fact, been a step forward. They were not only forbidden to leave the island, but they were forbidden to roam freely as they had in the past. And the "profits" that the Chilean government had promised to use to better the lot of the islanders became another of Easter's mysteries. What happened to all the money? In any case, the lot of the Pascuenses did not noticeably improve.

A year after the Chilean navy took over all governmental and sheep-raising operations on Easter, a celebrity arrived on the island. Not many personages from the outside world were known by every Pascuense. But they all knew of Señor Kon-Tiki. Indeed, some had tried to follow in his watery footsteps.

Seven years prior to his arrival on Easter, Thor Heyerdahl had made a voyage which was not only famed throughout the world, but which had caused quite a stir in the Navel of the World.

Heyerdahl and five other men had sailed on a balsa wood raft from Peru to the South Sea islands. They undertook this "suicide voyage" to prove Heyerdahl's impossible theory: that the most ancient of the peoples who inhabited the islands of Polynesia had originally lived in Peru before the Inca Indians ever got there. These people were unlike other Indians. They had white skin; the men grew long beards. They were taller people than the Incas. And some of them had red hair.

When the Spaniards first came to Peru, the Incas had told them about "white gods" who had lived in the land long ago, and who had erected colossal monuments. These white gods had been wise; they had been peaceful. They taught the Incas much about building huge stone structures, and about agriculture. But when the Incas came to power, the white gods suddenly left. They disappeared across the horizon of the Pacific.

Early Europeans who came to Polynesia found in the South Sea islands men and women who had very pale skin, reddish hair and beards—in striking contrast to the golden-brown, black-haired, beardless Polynesians. Heyerdahl was convinced that he had discovered the secret of where these pale, bearded Polynesians came from.

There was only one problem. How had they reached the South Sea islands—over 4,000 miles away—when the only sailing vessels they had were balsa-wood rafts?

Heyerdahl and the adventurous men who volunteered to go with him built a balsa-wood raft exactly according to the drawings left by Inca Indians. They named their raft *Kon-Tiki*. It was well known that Tiki was the great Polynesian chief god, son of the sun. But in his intensive research in Peruvian libraries, Heyerdahl had discovered that Tiki was the sun king of the red-haired white men who had—according to the Incas—"disappeared overseas to the westward."

Heyerdahl and his five raftmates had set out to "prove the possibility" that the Polynesian pale redheads had originally come from Peru. But even in the year 1947, the balsa-raft voyage seemed an utter impossibility, since those vast spaces of ocean through which they planned to sail lay outside all shipping routes and were virtually unknown.

Yet the men had made it. They sailed 4,200 nautical miles, a distance equal to that between Chicago and Moscow. And they made their voyage from Peru to Puka Puka in 101 days.

They did not go to Easter Island or anywhere near it—for they drifted along the Humbolt and South Equatorial currents, which carried them far to the north of Easter.

But the news of what they had done reached Easter, and

many Pascuenses promptly decided that if their ancestors had done it, and if Señor Kon-Tiki had done it, they too could do it. They need not remain imprisoned by the Chileans in a corner of their island. They need not remain imprisoned on the island itself because of the ocean distances. They could make rafts and reach Tahiti—which lay 2,600 miles away.

The fact that Easter was still nearly treeless put a damper on raft building. However some determined Pascuenses "borrowed" planks brought by the Chileans for building purposes. Secretly, they made small open boats—ostensibly for fishing. And a few did reach Tahiti—starving and three-quarters dead. The voyage was perilous, and the Chilean governor had been forced to install Chilean guards to watch over the newly built "fishing boats" in order to see that they never set out on an ocean voyage. (The governor had tried using native guards, but they had joined the would-be sailors and took off for Tahiti in the dead of night.)

Threats of imprisonment proved no deterrent at all to the would-be voyagers. They regarded the jail as a joke, or a vacation. In any case, it certainly was not an incarceration, as prisoners were sent home every day for their meals. This had proved a necessary step, for Pascuenses would proudly announce some crime they had committed—in order to be sent to prison where they could get free food.

When Señor Kon-Tiki's ship—a white, streamlined trawler —came to Easter Island in November 1955, the Chilean military governor was overjoyed. "Now," he exclaimed to Heyerdahl, "your ship can take over guard duty!"

The Norwegian was puzzled.

The governor explained the problem. "If I can tell the natives that we'll fetch them back with your ship if they start, I'll be free of all this watchkeeping."[2]

Heyerdahl laughed, and agreed. And the governor, in turn,

agreed that the archaeologists could do all the digging they wanted to, anywhere they wished on the island.

Heyerdahl, already an expert on the South Seas, had come with five expert archaeologists, a doctor, a photographer, a crew of thirteen, his wife, his teen-aged son, and his two-year-old daughter, Anette.

They remained on Easter for six months, the first people ever to do scientific archaeological digging. They not only proved that the island's most dramatic legend had, in fact, happened, but they found answers to some of the mysteries concerning the monoliths. And they discovered an island past and people which no one knew had ever existed.

When Señor Kon-Tiki arrived on the island, there was not one statue standing on its ahu; all had been toppled to the ground during the Statue-overthrowing Time. When Señor Kon-Tiki went away, he left behind an impressive souvenir of the expedition's stay: A giant *moai* stood on its altar at Anakena beach, looming over the landscape. It seemed to be staring—not only into the past, but into the future when other giant stone men would once again stand upright, silhouetted against the sky.

Without the detailed records of the Heyerdahl expedition and those of the men—and one woman—who came before him, virtually nothing could have been stated with certainty about the island's fascinating and mysterious Stone Age people.

Part II

The Stone Age Islanders

chapter 5

In every aspect of the exploration of the life and times of the ancient islanders, there is one overwhelming fact which must be kept continually in mind: the location of Easter Island. It is this which turns even so simple a sight as a butterfly into a mystery. As Pierre Loti put it in 1872: "And the butterflies, white and yellow butterflies; who was it that brought their spawn across eight hundred leagues of ocean?"

The Frenchman's words about the island's utter isolation can well be used as a backdrop and a framework for all that is to come:

> There exists in the midst of the great ocean, in a region where nobody goes, a mysterious and isolated island; no other land is near it and . . . in all directions empty and terrifying immensities surround it. . . .
> The region of the Pacific between America and Oceania is itself larger than the Atlantic Ocean; the widest marine solitude, the most frightening desert extent of ocean there is in our world. In the center lies Easter Island, unique, a tiny pebble in the middle of the ocean.[1]

Another factor should be well noted: the ancient islanders are not ancient in terms of the chronology of the outside world.

The islanders do not agree on many facts concerning their illustrious Stone Age ancestors. But on one matter they all concur: Their founding father was King Hotu Matua. However, there is no agreement among islanders, ethnologists, or anthropologists on when the great king came. The only certainty is that by the time Hotu Matua arrived on the isolated island, the Stone Age was a remnant of the far distant past in the outside world.

How were Hotu Matua's varied arrival dates determined? By the same means that other events of pre-recorded history are dated throughout Polynesia: the ancestor system. The natives on Easter could recount a long list of kings who were direct decendants of Hotu Matua. The list ended abruptly with King Kai Makoi who was carried off by the Peruvian slave traders in 1862. But the number of chiefs who came between Hotu Matua and Kai Makoi varied. Six such lists were obtained by outsiders who visited the island. The longest was compiled by Paymaster Thomson in 1886. It contained fifty-seven names. The shortest was made by Father Roussel in 1865. It contained only twenty-one names. Métraux's list was twenty to thirty.

Heyerdahl, in his scholarly tome, *The Archeology of Easter Island,* opts for the paymaster's line-up and, following the standard procedure among Polynesian ethnologists (twenty-five years to a generation), he concludes that Hotu Matua arrived about 450 A.D.

Father Sebastian, on the other hand, takes Métraux's list and points out that the kings usually transferred their power to their eldest son after a reign which averaged fifteen years. Consequently, Hotu Matua may have come in the sixteenth century.

In any case, whether he arrived in the fifth century or the sixteenth, he got there. And ever since, he has been the sole stellar light among the heroes of Easter Island. The first Europeans who were able to communicate with the islanders reported that the natives were incredulous to learn that Hotu Matua's name was unknown in the outside world.

Even as late as the mid-1950s—as Thor Heyerdahl reported in his book *Aku Aku*—natives spoke about Hotu Matua "as naturally as an Englishman would speak of Queen Victoria."

Did the great king really exist or was he merely made of the fabric of legends?

In the words of Father Sebastian: "I have no doubt that Hotu Matua is an historical figure and very likely came from the Marquesas Islands. Tradition says his home was an island called Hiva. In the Marquesas this word occurs in the names of three of the islands—Niku Hiva, Fatu Hiva, and Hiva Ova."[2]

Until Father Sebastian's death in January 1969, the priest was regarded as the greatest living authority on the subject of Easter Island. He was the island's official librarian and owned practically everything ever published in any language about Easter Island. He knew every expert who came there from the year 1935 to 1968, and he knew every aspect of their findings. He also knew all of the island legends. He firmly believed that there had been a great king named Hotu Matua, and virtually all other Easter Island experts agreed with him. But where legends ended and history began is a matter with no sharp dividing line.

The legends and songs about Hotu Matua were passed on through generations of islanders. There were many legends—as befits so notable a hero. But the ones which told most about the life and times of the great *ariki henua* were these:

Hotu Matua was a chief on an island called Hiva, which seems to have been a fine place—but too hot.

Hotu's younger brother Machaa, fell in love with a beautiful girl—who had also caught the eye and affection of another island chief, named Oroi.

The scheming young beauty promised to pledge herself to Oroi forever, if he could walk round the entire island of Hiva without stopping once to rest. While Oroi was trekking round the island, the girl ran off with Machaa—which led to a terrible tribal war between Oroi's people and those of Hotu Matua.

Hotu Matua's tribe lost the war. But Oroi did not get the girl. Instead, Hotu Matua, his brother, and girl friend, and some 300 followers set off in a huge double canoe to find a new land in which to settle. (The great god Make-Make had previously made known to Machaa in a dream "that a large uninhabited island could be found by steering toward the setting sun.")

Among Hotu Matua's many problems on the hazardous 120-day trip was his very pregnant wife—who started giving birth as soon as they sighted land. ("As the canoe passed Taharoa the vaginal mucus appeared; as it passed Hanga Hoonu the mucus plug was delivered, and upon arrival at Anakena the amniotic fluid flowed out." Father Sebastian translated the vivid biological details of the royal birth and then added: "It is unfortunate that many other aspects of the events of arrival were not remembered in similar detail.[3]

The double canoes were so large that there was room for a secret stowaway—none other than Oroi, who had given up all his duties and pleasures as chief on Hiva in order to take his revenge. He seems to have forgotten about his girl friend and Hotu Matua's brother. All his evil thoughts centered on the king. In the dead of night, he crept out of the canoe—and disappeared up the beach and into the darkness. He would bide his time before striking.

Meanwhile, Hotu Matua, his wife, and new baby boy, lived

in the cave of the Kena bird while the master builder, Neku Kehu, set about building a fine stone house fit for a king—with another house beside it for the queen and crying child, and an outside kitchen with a huge five-sided oven.

The style developed by Neku Kehu for the royal residences was unique in all the world and was used by the natives of Easter Island until the 1860s when Brother Eugène persuaded the natives to move from their dwellings—scattered all over the island—to form a village of huts clustered around his church at Hanga-roa.

Forster, the naturalist who came with Captain Cook in 1774, described the "boat houses" thus:

> The foundation consists of stones about a foot long, laid level with the surface in two curved lines converging at the extremities. These lines were about six feet asunder in the middle, but not above one foot at the ends. In every stone of this foundation we observed one or two holes, in each of which a stake was inserted.[4]

The stakes, or branches, which were stuck in the holes, were then bent to meet in an arched roof foundation. Reeds woven through this framework formed walls and ceilings. The finished house had the shape of a canoe. It was often the size of a canoe as well.

As further embellishment, there was usually a crescent-shaped "front porch" made of smooth, rounded stones. Sometimes small stones—or even statues—were placed at either side of the door.

Why the boat-shaped houses struck the fancy of the islanders is another mystery. They could not have provided much comfort. They had no windows and the roof was so low it was impossible to stand up inside.

Such a dwelling might have been fine for Hotu Matua, for,

The Stone Age islanders lived in boat-shaped houses. Wooden poles stuck in foundation-stone holes were woven through with totora reeds to form windowless walls and ceiling. Carved stone figures by stone-cobbled porch frightened off evil spirits.

presumably, he lived in it alone. But the natives who copied this house style crowded in as many as the place could possibly hold each night.

Pierre Loti entered many of the boat-shaped houses. He described the two finest ones, each of which belonged to a chief.

> An old tattooed man, wearing long black feathers stuck on his head, undoubtedly some chief . . . invites me in. I have to do this on all fours like a cat going through a cat door, since the entrance, level with the earth and guarded by two divinities of evil aspect, is a round hole hardly two feet high.
> Inside it's impossible to see a thing on account of the crowd pressing all around, there is no way of standing up; especially after the vivifying air out of doors, it is hard to breathe. The place smells like a tannery.

The next day he longed for a siesta:

> But where to find a little shade for my head in a country where there's not a tree, not a green bush. After some hesitation I go to ask the old chief a moment's hospitality, crawling into his lodging. The place is very warm and encumbered with stretched out bodies. Under this turtle shell, which is exactly like an overturned canoe, the chief lives with his family: one wife, two sons, a daughter, a son-in-law, a grandson, plus rabbits and chickens and seven mean cats. . . . They make room for me on the carpet of woven reeds.
> In this small space, hardly a meter and a half high [five feet] and forty meters long [fourteen feet] a thousand things are carefully suspended; little idols of black wood which are engraved with coarse enamelling, lanced with points of sharpened obsidian, paddles carved with human figures, feather headdresses, ornaments for the dance or for combat and some utensils of various shapes, of use unknown to me, which all seem extremely ancient.

Our ancestors of the first ages, when they were risking the first emergence from the caves, must have built huts like this, ornamented with similar objects: one feels here a type of humanity infinitely primitive and one might say younger than our twenty or thirty thousand years.[5]

Loti wrote those on-the-spot notes in the year 1872. This was during the destructive Statue-Over-Throwing-Time when warriors and cannibals reigned on the island, and people were accustomed to hiding out for months in caves. The boat-shaped houses were, presumably, as comfortable as a cave.

The remarkable prehistoric islanders who had built the stupendous stone monoliths had lived in times of peace, yet, even they favored the boat-shaped houses. Another mystery: Why, when they could produce miracles of stone construction as evidenced in the ahus, or altars—some of which were fourteen feet high and almost 500 feet long—why, when—without knowledge of the wheel or any engineering devices—they had dragged the giant statues, unscathed, across stony fields to set them up on these ahus . . . why, when they could perform such impossible building feats as raising a ten-ton topknot to rest on the head of a statue three stories high . . . *why* did they not trouble to make themselves better dwellings than these low, crowded, hot, stinking boat-shaped houses?

There was never a surplus of anything on the island, with a single exception: stones. And, indeed, some islanders did build themselves houses of stone. But these were not the comfortable, cool, commodious many-roomed dwellings which they could have constructed. They looked like a pile of stones. A typical one was twenty-four feet long, four to seven feet high, six feet wide—with a square two-foot entryway which also served as the sole window.

The stone houses, crude though they were, at least had

thick walls and were, therefore, cooler than the reed-covered huts. Nevertheless, it was the boat-shaped houses which reigned supreme for centuries as the most popular architectural style on the island.

Certainly, when Hotu Matua's master builder constructed his dwelling for the king, he could never have imagined what an all-pervading influence this new house style would have.

He also built a special arcade on the royal beach. A broad avenue, made of tall sticks topped by garlands of feathers, led down to the sea. Only the King, his queens, their children, and servants were entitled to use this beach. Anyone else who dared venture onto Anakena was killed.

King Hotu Matua presumably spent much time swimming at Anakena. No one expected him to take part in the hard work involved in colonizing the island. The ariki henua was not even expected to rule. His head was heavily endowed with *mana*—a supernatural power which could bring good luck to his followers. And that was all they required of him: an active use of his mana.

The king's mana had certainly manifested itself on the long voyage from Hiva.

One of the most strategic elements of such a voyage was the survival of the seedlings and roots which the colonizers brought in their canoes. Their new land—if they ever found it—might be completely barren. Their future existence might well depend on the fragile life in the uprooted plantings. What varieties of fruits, trees, and vegetables were lost en route from Hiva, or after arrival on Easter, the legends do not recount. But the King's mana must have worked magnificently when it came to the matter of sweet potatoes. They flourished, as did their close relatives, yams and taro. Indeed, the islanders eventually developed twenty-five varieties of sweet potatoes.

Roggoveen reported that he had received piles of sweet potatoes as gifts. Captain Cook's party found sweet potatoes in "extensive plantations." And in 1864, Brother Eugène wrote in some despair of "the eternal sweet potatoes. It is the every day dish, the invariable staple food of the natives, big and small . . . the uniformity is perfect; always sweet potatoes, everywhere sweet potatoes."

Métraux reports a single-sentence summation of life by an island woman in 1934: "Here we begin at birth by eating sweet potatoes, then we go on eating sweet potatoes, and finally we die."

According to island legend, King Hotu Matua's people established other growing things: bananas, sugar cane, and *ti* (a plant with molasses-sweet roots); also gourds. (As late as 1889 Paymaster Thompson wrote: "A wild gourd constitutes the *only* water-jug and domestic utensil known to the natives. These calabashes grow in profusion on the island.")

Another useful item reputedly responsive to King Hotu's mana was the paper mulberry tree. For centuries, natives used the bark of this tree as their only source of clothing. They pounded the bark into thin sheets, which they sewed and wove together with fiber thread and needles made of fish or human bone. They used this tapa cloth for cloaks which doubled as blankets on the cool winter (June through September) night, and for loincloths, which men and women wore on occasion. Otherwise, there was not much call for the tapa cloth as people settled the clothing problem by rarely wearing any.

It is also reported in legends that Hotu Matua brought the totora reed, which was used for everything from making canoes to wrapping up corpses.

The other plant brought by Hotu Matua was the dwarf toromiro tree, which the islanders have always used for their remarkable wood carving—the sole ancient art form which still flourishes on the island today.

Finally, Hotu Matua brought the black rat (considered a delicacy by the ancient islanders) and the chicken. The fowl not only provided food but later proved to be the prevailing currency of this small and isolated realm.

The remains of many prehistoric chicken houses can still be seen. These structures looked more comfortable than the huts which housed the humans. They were built of heavy stone masonry with ceilings seven feet high. How was it known they were not used by humans? Because the entrance was only big enough for a chicken to enter. (This small doorway and the fortresslike walls presumably discouraged chicken thieves who might prowl about in the nighttime.)

Although the diet of the early islanders may not have been well-rounded, there was, at least, enough to eat. Even in times of severe drought when most of the plants died, there was always fish, including large and succulent crayfish which could be caught by hand at the island's few beaches.

But the real problem—from the very beginning—was water.

Even the great king's mana did not seem to be able to supply his thirsty people with sufficient water. And Hotu Matua pondered long on this problem.

The island's only constant supply of fresh water was found in the deep crater lakes of the three volcanoes. These lakes were covered near shore by thick, shaking bogs; the stagnant water, was far from delectable. Furthermore, fetching it meant clambering up one steep side of a volcano—slipping, sliding down the sharp-dropping crater's interior to reach the lake— then reversing the process, trying not to spill the few gourdsful of water which had been collected. The results were scarcely worth the effort.

Aside from the dreaded periods of drought, the rainfall was sufficient to keep crops alive. (Rain tends to come in short, intense showers which cover only one part of the island at a time. The average annual rainfall is forty-nine inches.)

But the problem lay in what happened to the rain when it did fall. It disappeared.

Easter Island has been described as a huge pumice stone, so riddled is it with underground caves. This image applies also to the island's volcanic soil which is so porous that rain quickly seeps through and disappears—which is why there is not so much as a single brook on all of the Easter Island.

Hotu Matua pondered this matter. What happened to the fresh water after it had vanished into the stony fields? Perhaps it met deep layers of rock which it could not penetrate. If this were so, the underground lake must empty somehow, somewhere. He explored the coastline looking closely for rivulets of fresh water which might run out from an underground lake and empty into the sea. And he found some. Most of the thin trickles of fresh water which ran from the rocks were, in fact, below sea level—and salt water, therefore, contaminated the fresh. Even those shallow pools of fresh water slightly above sea level were subject to being washed over by high waves. But perhaps something could be done.

The great king ordered that stone walls be built around the fresh-water coastal pools in an effort to keep the ocean out. This served less to keep the ocean out than to keep the fresh water in. Stone-lined wells at low-lying spots along the coast had the same results. But the water—though somewhat salty —was drinkable. (At least, the islanders thought so. The eighteenth-century seamen who tasted it thought they were being served brine.)

In any case, Hotu Matua's followers were understandably overjoyed at the fact that they no longer needed to go about parched with thirst. The brackish wells also enabled them to spread out and start new settlements around the seacoast.

Meanwhile, as the colonists were settling in, the villain Oroi was hiding out—biding his time until he could seek a suitable revenge.

He bided quite a time; years, in fact. Hotu Matua's wives bore him several sons. One day, the young princes were asleep in the sun, having tired themselves out by swimming off the rocks in a deserted cove. Then—according to the legend— Oroi crept up to them and killed them by sticking a crayfish's tail into their behinds.

In the evening when his sons did not come home, the King went out to look for them. When he found their bodies, he examined them closely and cried out, "O Oroi, you have crossed the seas to continue your war, for I recognize your hand." He wept bitterly and vowed revenge.

A year went by. Hotu Matua played the role of a great king. He traveled over the island, visiting the new villages, taking part in feasts and festivals, teaching his people the chants of their ancestors from Hiva. But he had a double reason for traveling; everywhere he went, he looked for Oroi.

One day, Oroi made a rope and stretched it across the path when the king was coming across a grassy field. Hotu Matua fell and pretended to be hurt. But when Oroi sprang at him, to kill him, the king raised his club and split Oroi's skull.

The villain's body was placed in an *umu*—to be baked before it was eaten. But since he, too, had been a chief on Hiva, Oroi's flesh would not burn, so they had to take him out of the oven and bury him at an ahu—which still bears his name.

Hotu Matua fathered four more sons and, when he grew old, he called them all to him and divided the island among them. Henceforth, each son would not only have his own land, but his own group of followers, or kin group—and so the social system of the island was started.

Finally, feeling death drawing close, Hotu Matua sent a servant to bring him water from a well which the king himself had dug at Huareva. It was not that he was thirsty. Were it only this, he could have asked for water from the crater lake of Rano Kau, which was much closer. The water was a symbol: He had solved his people's most pressing problem.

Then the ailing king dragged himself up to the edge of the Rano Kau crater. At the top of the precipice, he stood looking out at the ocean, supporting himself between two rocky points (which are still pointed out today). He begged the spirits— the *akuaku*—to let him hear once more the cry of the rooster of his homeland, Hiva. And from the far distance came the faint sound *"o'oa take heuheu"*—which is the way roosters cry in Hiva, as well as on Easter Island.

His sons built a tomb for him near the Bay of Akahanga. It was a simple tomb, made of earth and stones. Despite the massive mausoleums built later as burial places for lesser men, no one ever erected any other ahu for the island's greatest hero, the ariki henua Hotu Matua.

chapter 6

There is one fact which continues to be in dispute among Easter Islanders and outside experts: the ear-lobe length of Hotu Matua and his followers.

This might seem, at first glance, to be a minor matter. It is not. Indeed, ear length might be considered the single most important backbone fact of Easter's ancient history.

All the legends—as well as reports given by elderly natives to visiting experts—agree on one single matter: At the time of the Stone Age golden age when the great statues were built, there were two different groups of people who lived on the island—the Long Ears and the Short Ears. And the disaster which ended the golden age was the result of a dire war between them: a war of annihilation.

There are many who claim that Hotu Matua's people were the Long Ears. Those who insist that the great king came originally from the Marquesas point out that the custom of lengthening ear lobes existed in those islands as well.

Others are certain that the statue builders came from Peru. And there too (according to records made by the early Spanish conquerors) the Inca rulers were called *orejones,* or long ears, because they had artificially lengthened ear lobes—in contrast to their short-eared subjects.

Still others claim that Hotu Matua's people did not diddle with their ear lobes. They were Short Ears. The Long Ears came later.

Father Sebastian, after reading what all the experts had to say on the matter, and listening for years to all the varied legends, turned, as his most reliable source, to a leper.

A priest who truly tended the needs of his people—all of them—Father Sebastian came regularly to the dilapidated and stinking leprosarium which still existed on the island in the 1930s. There he was surrounded by some twenty men and women in various stages of decay. One of the lepers was a man named Arturo Teao who had entered the place as a youth, when the leprosarium was inhabited only by a few very old men. Since Arturo was keenly interested, the old lepers spent much time telling the young man everything that they had been told, and all that they themselves remembered of the old ways of life on the island. Eventually, all the old men died and Arturo became the only one to retain this knowledge.

Arturo Teao's version of the coming of the Long Ears was this:

Some time after Hotu Matua's people were well established on the island, new arrivals came in canoes. They were large, heavy-set men and Hotu Matua's people called them *Hanau Eepe*—*hanau* meaning people, and *eepe* meaning "heavy-set." Strangely eepe is a pun when said aloud, for *epe* means ear lobe. And this *was* the most notable single amazement about the new arrivals: Their ear lobes dangled down to their shoulders.

The Hanau Eepe achieved their lengthy lobes by piercing them and inserting ever-larger bone or wooden disks into them. Finally, a roll of tree bark was worn which acted as an ever-active spring continuing to stretch the opening—until the ear lobes had been converted into long cords which hung down to the shoulders.

The new long-eared immigrants did not seem to come as colonizers—but as explorers. They brought no women with them. They intermarried with the Short Ears. Their children however, took on the distinctive long-eared look.

Which ear-lengthed people came first and when they arrived is a matter of continuing interest and debate. But what is truly important and undeniable is what the Long Ears and Short Ears created when they got together.

We do not know when it started, but probably sometime between the ninth and the twelfth centuries the remarkable statue building began.

And with the statues came more mysteries.

The statues are unique. Statues had been made on other islands, other continents, by prehistoric peoples. But nowhere have they been found in the size and numbers as the mammoth moai (statues) on Easter Island. Nearly 1,000 moai were made. (At many times during the island's history the population of stone men far outnumbered the human population.)

They looked like no other statues ever created in any other land. Each resembled the other; yet, each was slightly different.

Their heads were long, rectangular-shaped. Their brows sloped back. Their eyes were set in deep-shadowed sockets, giving each figure a thoughtful, mysterious, somber mien— which changed according to where the sun sat in the sky.

Their ear lobes were long—which suggests that the Long Ears were the chief sculptors, with the Short Ears doing the more menial jobs—of which there were many.

Noses, too, were long and sometimes slightly concave. But even those with tip-tilted noses somehow managed to look somber.

The mouth of each statue was always the same: purse-lipped, disdainful, grim. Any human would feel small enough when standing before one of these stone giants, but the disapproving set of the thin lips could only serve to make a mere mortal feel smaller still.

The statues had torsos but no legs. As befitted these symbols of the island called the Navel of the World, each had a prominent navel. And each had arms which hung stiffly at the sides. Some had long, slender carefully carved fingers which turned toward each other across the lower part of the statue's slightly potbelly.

Some were better made than others—and these generally had backs which were carved in designs which represented tattooing. Some were crudely made, but even they transmitted the brooding, almost frightening mood of ever-watchful supernatural beings.

Yet, these stone giants were not gods. Each had a name—which was passed on down through the generations. But the name was never that of a god. It was thought to be that of a great ancestor of the kin group that inhabited the locality in which the stone man stood. The islanders referred to all the statues as *aringa ora*—"living faces."

Some of the statues were small, relatively speaking, with a nose as long as a man is tall. But some stretched to fifty and sixty feet and weighed up to ninety tons. The shorter statues were perhaps the most ancient, for it seems that at the height of the golden age, the kin groups were driven by a spirit of competition: Which area could produce the hugest stone ancestor?

Of all the mysteries concerning the moai there is one matter which is startlingly clear: how they were made. And that, paradoxically, presents the most shattering mystery of all: Why, at the very height of the statue-making period, did it all suddenly stop? Why did the carvers throw down their small stone picks and leave, never to return to statuemaking again? The picks they dropped in haste when they ran away have been picked up by the thousands as visitors came to view this site throughout the centuries. But many thousands more rock-chipping picks still remain—eloquent evidence that something happened suddenly to end it all.

A few of the stone giants found here and there around the island were made of basalt rock. But all the rest were fashioned from the same hard yellow-gray, black-grained stone—found only in one place on Easter: the volcano crater of Rano Raraku near the eastern end of the island.

This site is one of the most remarkable in the world, and will always remain so. It has not changed since the statue-makers ran away. The savage cannibals who later roamed the island destroying the standing statues, inflicted no damage on the stone men of Rano Raraku. This place will remain as an eternal testimonial to the incredible achievements of the pre-historic men of Easter Island.

The site is striking, even from the far distance: The great volcano of Rano Raraku humps against the horizon like a slumbering whale.

Upon closer view, the statues, telescoped by perspective, seem to be merely a scattering of dark specks on the grass-covered southwest slope of the volcano.

But, upon entering their realm, the brooding guardians of the statues' birthplace loom large. Over seventy of them; huge bodyless heads staring from deep-welled eyeless, sockets.

It is not the immense size of the heads which overwhelms so much as their expression; the orchestrated symphony of stares from cynical, disdainful, disapproving stone giants.

Some, it is true, have a more sympathetic mien, particularly the head with the notably upturned nose whom the natives chummily call the Pascuense equivalent of Stinky.

Their bodies buried, over seventy huge heads stand guard at the foot of Rano Raraku, where the monoliths were made.

But as a group, they are mysterious, awesome, and as Pierre Loti wrote in 1872:

> They frighten. . . . The meridian sun blasts them, the tropical sun which exaggerates their harsh expression, putting more black in their sockets. . . . The slope of the terrain makes their shadows long on this graveyard grass.

But unforgettable as the view of these bodyless giants may be, an even more incredible sight awaits one at Rano Raraku on the rearing southern wall of the volcano crater.

What seemed at first to be a long, shadowed boulder is, in fact, a partially hacked-out stone giant.

Then the eye picks out other shapes from the cliffside: tier upon tier of monolithic stone mummies. Most lie prone, but some stand straight as though leaning back against the cliff. Others tilt to the left or right. And a few are standing on their heads.

Some are in the embryo stage with only the indication of features and torso chipped from the yellow-gray volcanic stuff. Some have half-finished face and chest—grotesque, malformed. Some are finished, with only a ridge of rock attaching the statue to the cliffside. And there are many empty crypts, the birthplace of giants who have been cut loose and transported—somehow—down the mountain.

Ascending this steep slope is perhaps the strangest mountain climb in the world: standing on a ledge of pursed lips, crawling over a cheek, sitting on an eyebrow, or lying down to rest on a smooth ridge which is a giant's nose.

At the top of the precipice—five hundred feet above the grassy plain—are more stone men, on their backs, staring eternally at the sky with sightless eyes. And on the inner cliff of the volcano are still more of them: many standing, but still attached to the rock; some prone, sleep forever in a canopied bed of stone. And some have slid down the precipice to the shore of the crater lake below.

They vary in size, though each is huge. The longest is sixty-nine feet. He is unfinished and lies aslant; standing upright, he would be taller than a six-story building.

Over 200 statues have been counted in this quarry, in various stages of creation. More lie buried by landslides of rock and rubble.

What pulsing activity this represents; what fantastic organization of island society.

Early visitors who did not get to the quarry no doubt

Islander at Rano Raraku quarry observes prone statue carved by his Stone Age ancestors.

assumed that the statues were made one by one, through the decades. But here at Ranu Raraku the evidence shouts out: The ancient islanders were caught up in a compulsion of creating stone statues. Not one, nor a dozen were made at a time, but several hundred at once.

The picks which were used to make these monoliths were small pieces of hard black obsidian, a rock which is rare in the islands of the Pacific. A small volcanic cone on the southwest side of the island is called Orito. It is not composed of volcanic ash like the other cones. It is made of black obsidian. If the black obsidian rock of Orito had not been found on this desolate island, the giant stone men could never have been created.

Here (½ their actual size) are some of the obsidian picks used by the statuemakers.

Islanders carved the giant stone statues with small crude picks made of hard black obsidian.

At first look, it seems easy enough to see how the statues were made. But many visitors—starting with an eighteenth-century Spanish seaman—did more than have a first look. As Don Francisco Antonio de Agüera y Infanzon wrote in 1770: "The material of the statue is very hard stone, and therefore weighty; having tried it myself with a hoe it struck fire: a proof of its density."

Many later visitors tried hitting the hard rock with one of the obsidian picks which was lying on the ground. All they achieved was a little dust; they made no mark on the stone at all. But given the fact that the statue carvers did find a way to carve this hard mountain rock with no tools other than still-harder rock picks, it is at least easy to see all the steps involved in statuemaking. The "exhibit" is on display for eternity at the Ranu Raraku quarry.

The face was made first, and the front of the body. Ridges

were then hacked out at the sides so that the long ears could be cut, and the arms; then the long-fingered hands, and the navel. Details were added to many of the stone men; tapered fingernails, ornaments to lengthen the ears. (But one detail was always omitted; the eyes. The statues remained blind till they got to where they were going. Only then were the pupils made.)

Finally, before being moved from its birthplace, each statue was carefully rubbed with pumice stone, and polished.

Why not see to the details and polishing when the statue stood in its final resting place? The workers would then not need to take such care when lowering the monolith down the cliffside. Another mystery with no answer.

In any case, when the giant was decreed to be finished, the wedge of stone which still attached him to the rock was chipped away. He was now free to be moved. Those which were made on the inside of the volcano cliff had first to be hauled to the top, and then slid down to the plains far below —all without marring the details already carved, and without destroying other statues being carved from the cliffside.

But how?

Paymaster Thomson puzzled out the problem this way when he visited Ranu Raraku in 1886:

> The work of lowering the huge images from the upper terraces to the bottom of the crater and thence over the wall and down into the plain below was of great magnitude, and we are lost in wonder that so much could be accomplished by rude savages ignorant of everything in the way of mechanical appliances. The average weight of these statues would be something between 10 and 12 tons, but some are very large and would weight over 40 tons. It is possible that a slide was made, upon which the images were launched to the level ground below. . . .[1]

Such was Thomson's solution for the statues he had seen on the southern side of the volcano. But, like many before and after him who arrived at "satisfactory solutions," further investigation ended only in complete bafflement. The next morning the paymaster:

> . . . visited the image-builders' workshops on the west side of Rano Raraku, which are much more extensive than those on the inside of the crater. These workshops commence well up on the side of the mountain and extend quite to the summit by irregular terraces. In places these terraces extend one above the other with unfinished images upon each, and the configuration of the land is such as to preclude all idea of launching the statues by means of a slide. We were unable to arrive at any satisfactory conclusion as to how the immense statues on the upper tier of works could be moved to the plain below.[2]

But whatever the answer as to how the stone men were moved from their birthplace, they somehow arrived at the bottom slope of the cliff. There the "rude savages" had collected high piles of stone splinters, carried down from the quarry. Each statue which descended was then—somehow— set into a hole dug for it in the rubble. Propped up in place, the final work was done on the back which was scarred by the final removal from the ridge of stone that held it to the cliffside. Some of the huge backs were decorated with designs, and many statues were adorned with a belt of carved symbols.

Then the statues awaited transportation around the island. The stone heads which seem to guard the quarry are, in fact, finished moai all ready to be moved to an altar elsewhere on the island. Each had been set in a hole by the statuemakers so that the final carving could be done. Then—the catastrophe struck. The carvers ran away. The sands of time, quite literally, filled in the hole made for each statue and grasses formed a collar around each neck. These moai will wait at the foot of Rano Raraku throughout eternity. Others—in the process of being moved—lie face in the dirt along the ancient roadways: Long, yellowish-gray shapes, they can be spotted easily, for rock of this distinctive coloring is found only in the Rano Raraku quarry.

Some moai lie alone. Some are in groups of two or three. All were transported across the island face downward. Paymaster Thomson was one of the many who made a puzzled note of this: "Why they were dragged over the ground face downward instead of upon their backs thus protecting their features, is a mystery yet unsolved."[3]

But the greatest mysteries of all were still to come.

How was a statue raised onto its ahu? Some of the altars were as much as fifteen feet high.

And *how* was a heavy stone topknot then put onto its head?

chapter 7

Some seven miles from the statues' birthplace, Rano Rara-ku, lies a small volcano called Puna Pau. It is distinctive for one reason. Its deep interior looks as though it has been soaked in blood.

It also is pockmarked with huge cylindrical holes.

This is the quarry of the red topknots.

Not all of the statues were adorned with them. But many were.

And activity here stopped as suddenly as it did on Rano Raraku. Six finished topknots still lie inside the crater. Others had—somehow—been pulled up the steep slope to the edge of Puna Pau, where they wait to be taken further. Some were en route. They have lain for centuries, abandoned in a field.

They do not vary in style, only in size. The smallest are a mere two tons. The average weigh in at ten tons. The largest one weighs thirty tons. Why would the islanders want to carve a thirty-ton topknot? It must have been designed for the head of the most monstrously tall moai of all. And how did the natives ever plan to get it up there?

Another question remains: why red topknots, and why only on some of the statues? (Twenty-five topknots lie in or near the quarry. Fifty-eight lie close to the statues they once adorned.)

According to the records of Roggoveen, Captain Cook, and others, some of the naked natives they saw had white skin and red hair. It also seemed to the early explorers that these natives were held in high esteem by the others. Indeed, red hair sems to have been such a highly valued item that, at a later date, some dark-haired natives dyed their locks red. In 1872, Pierre Loti described the first Easter Islander he encountered:

> His skin of a reddish copper color, is ornamented with blue tattooing; his hair is of an artificial red bound up with scabiosa stems to the top of his head forming a red pompadour which the wind stirs like a flame.

A crewman on Captain Cook's ship drew a native with this typical topknot hairstyle (worn, incidentally by brunettes as well as redheads).

Why this veneration for red hair?

Perhaps because the original redheads were the ancestors who also had white skin. And the veneration for pale skins persisted from ancient times into the twentieth century. The pale-skinned natives were called *oho-tea,* or the "light-haired."

So sought after was this pale skin that, up until the time of the smallpox epidemic in 1863, the tradition of the *neru* virgins persisted. A young girl who was fortunate (or unfortunate) enough to be born with pale skin was put with her white-skinned island sisters in a cave, in order to be shut away from the sun and remain as pale as possible. These neru virgins were allowed out only for special religious festivals when they had their "moment in the sun" and reigned as white-skinned princesses. Then back they went to their cave, called *Ana o Keke,* "Cave of the Sun's Inclination."

This volcanic island is riddled with caves. But Ana o Keke is one of the least accessible. To find it, one must drop down from the top of a precipice on Poike Peninsula to a narrow rock ledge six hundred feet above breakers which pound against black boulders. The sea wind, blocked by the precipice, whips and roars against the slender ledge. One wonders how many neru virgins were blown away before they ever reached their holy cave.

Nor is the cave itself any happy haven. It is necessary to squeeze through the narrow opening—which not only keeps out intruders, but light.

The cave is less than five feet high, and so narrow the virgins would have had to squat in rows against each wall. It could uncomfortably accommodate only a dozen of them. There is a back room, somewhat more spacious, where the virgins could at least stand up and stretch. But in order to get there, it was necessary for a girl to inch along on her belly through a narrow, chilly, muddy, and perilous passage, four hundred feet long.

Each neru virgin spent months in this cave—all for the glory of pale skin. Aside from the religious festivals when they had their outings, they saw only the women who had been appointed to bring them food. When smallpox swept the island, the neru virgins were so isolated from the rest of the community that they did not catch the disease. But there was no one to bring them food; so, they starved to death.

The cult of the neru virgins makes it dramatically clear that pale skin was much revered.

Until the advent of hair dyeing on the island, red hair almost invariably went with white skin. Since each giant statue represented an actual ancestor of a certain kin group, the people who had been fortunate enough to have a white-skinned redhead as an illustrious ancestor would understandably have felt it worth all the trouble of carving, moving, and mounting a red stone topknot on *their* statue, in order to proclaim this proud lineage far and wide.

Who were these kin groups? How did they operate—and cooperate—in order to produce the amazing moai?

According to island legend, they started when Hotu Matua divided the island among his sons. The oldest son inherited the title of ariki-mau (king) and received the stretch of coastal land between Anakena and Tea tea. The second son, Miru, was given land between Anakena and Hanga-roa. The rest of the island was divided between the four remaining royal sons.

In the next generation, this land became subdivided. A legend about Miru's tribe indicates one way in which this happened. In one of the wars, Miru's people suffered great losses. But two of Miru's direct descendants escaped; one was named Taka, the other Parapuna. Taka's wife gave birth to a baby, at which point Taka passed his wife on to Parapuna. And when she bore *him* a child, she was sent back to Taka. The Miru woman was kept busy rotating between Taka and Parapuna, until she had produced a supply of sons and daughters for each. Taka and Parapuna then formed two subtribes, or kin groups—all of whom were directly descended from the royal ancestor, Miru.

The most important kin groups had oceanfront property. Those lowest on the social scale had land in the *uta*—the center of the island. (The uta was also the realm of the aku aku —island spirits, some of whom were friendly, some mischievous, and some downright malicious.)

This allocation of land according to social strata no doubt accounts for the reason that almost all of the ahu and moai were set up by the sea.

The kin groups during the golden age of statue building must have lived under the twin banners of cooperation and competition, with a notable absence of conflict. Otherwise, it would have been impossible for an island population, which could not have exceeded 4,000, to create so many remarkable stone giants. A quarry where 200 statues were being made at the same time, meant a well-ordered social structure throughout the entire island.

There were those who cooked for the quarry workers—payment for the hard labor of chipping and hauling the stone men was in the currency of food: cooked food, made in the many *umu tahus*—earth ovens—around in the quarry.

There must have been many hundreds of people who worked in and around the quarry from dawn to dusk. Many hundreds more were involved in the task of transporting the giants and building, or rebuilding, the ahus. The rest of the population worked to support these workers. There were the *tangata heuheu henua*: the farmers; and the *tangata tere vaka*: the fishermen.

No one, it seems, was forced to work at his job. There were no slaves. The stern-faced statues were not produced by men who worked under the whiplash, or in fear.

It was a time of intense productivity in all areas of island life. But, like every golden age, it was destined to come to an end. In the Navel of the World, however, the end was not any gradual decline and fall. It came suddenly; in one drastic day.

chapter 8

No one knows why it came, or when the rumblings began. But an island legend seems to hold much truth to anyone who walks around on Poike Peninsula.

According to this version of island history, passed on through the generations, the Long Ears thought of a fine idea: They would rid the island of stones and make planting easier, and they would achieve this noble end by getting the Short Ears to pick up all the stones and throw them into the ocean. They ordered the Short Ears to start this project at Poike Peninsula. And presumably, the Short Ears did set out to do the Long Ears' bidding. In any case, the slopes of Poike present the only landscape on the island which is notably clear of rocks and stones.

After doing a job on Poike, the Short Ears rebelled. "We discovered this island," they declared. "Our great King Hotu Matua was a Short Ears. We will not give our island to you."

Since the Long Ears paid no attention, the Short Ears decided to kill them all. Then the island would—quite properly —belong to the Short Ears alone.

The Long Ears, getting wind of this rebellion, decided to move hastily to Poike Peninsula.

Why Poike?

A look at the map makes it evident. The three shores of the peninsula are comprised entirely of sheer high cliffs. It would be virtually impossible for an enemy to land by boat and climb the precipices. Therefore, the Long Ears did not need to trouble defending their back and rear flanks.

The only easy access to Poike is across the western slope. And any movement of Short Ears across the plain to Poike could easily be spotted by Long-eared watchmen stationed on the volcano, which rises gradually to some 1,300 feet above sea level.

To make their natural fortress still more secure, the Long Ears dug a deep trench—about sixteen feet wide and twelve feet deep. It stretched for two miles across the base of the peninsula. It was made in twenty-six sections, with short spaces in between. The rocks and earth which were dug up to make the trench were used as further fortification—a steep slope on the Poike side. Then the Long Ears placed wood, dry reeds, and other flammable material in the trenches.

They had, they believed, a fine defense system. Should the Short Ears be spotted moving over the plains to Poike, the ditches would be ignited. The advancing armies would first have to face a wall of fire, and then the Long Ears who crouched behind the hill of rubble on the other side of the ditch.

It might have worked out just this way—were it not for a woman.

Her name was Moko Pingei, and she lived on Poike with her Long-eared husband. But Moko was a Short Ears—more loyal to her people than to her spouse. One night she crept past the sleeping sentries, made her way along the edge of the trench by the cliff, and ran through the darkness until she met some Short Ears. Then she arranged a secret plan.

Short-eared spies should hang about near the Poike Ditch.

If, one evening, they saw Moko sitting at the edge of the ditch weaving a basket, this would mean that the coast was reasonably clear—whereupon the rest of the maneuver would be put into action.

And it happened exactly according to plan.

One moonless night, a host of Short Ears—alerted by the basket-weaving Moko—slunk silently, one by one, around each cliff-side border of the trench and hid themselves behind boulders at the edges of the peninsula. At dawn, a troop of Short Ears, with much diversionary shouting and yelling, came charging over the plain toward the Poike Ditch.

Long-eared defenders ran down to the ditch, and set it alight. Then they squatted behind the high mounds of earth, waiting for the charge of the Short Ears, which did not come. At least, it did not come from the plains.

Meanwhile, the Short Ears, who had sneaked across the border the previous night, came out of hiding and—in pincer formation—converged on the Long Ears.

Too late, the Long Ears realized what was happening. The Short Ears were masters of the mountainside. They swept the Long Ears before them—every last man, woman, and child— straight toward the ditch where searing flames speared high into the air.

Then, according to legend, "They threw the Hanau Eepe into the trenches. As if they were stones they threw them down into the fires. The Hanau Eepe were finished. They died. The trenches were filled and the good odor of the cooked meat of the Hanau Eepe rose into the air."

Only three Long Ears managed to escape being burned alive. They hid in a cave. But they were shortly discovered by the Short Ears, who killed two of them. The third, however, seems to have had a silver tongue or exceptionally moving shrieks and cries. In any case, the Short Ears decided: "We will leave him unharmed and he may have many descendants."

The sole surviving Long Ears was called Ororoina. He married a Short Ears, and did have many descendants. In fact, he had so many that the Short Ears became worried. Consequently, they decided to return to the initial formula: Only one Long Ears should remain alive. All the descendants were put into a hut. The entrance was sealed up. And the thatch was set afire.

The Long Ears suffocated. A grandson of Ororoina was the one Long Ears to remain alive. He married a Short Ears, and had a son named Inaki Uhi. He begat Ao Ngatu, who begat Hare Kai Hiva—who was baptized by Brother Eugène, and given the Christian name Adam (which the islanders translated as Atamu. Atamu spawned one of the most proliferous families on the island today. They now have the surname Atan, or Atam, and are respected as the only genuine Long-eared descendants on Easter Island today.

There are numerous nongenuine Long-eared descendants, for after the annihilation of all Long Ears but Ororoina, the Short Ears decided to take up the custom of lengthening *their* lobes. This they did—which is why all the eighteenth- and nineteenth-century visitors to the island saw so many natives with shoulder-length ear lobes.

The fact that Ororoina's lineage can be traced so accurately enabled the islanders to count back and set a very specific date for the Poike Ditch fire.

Allowing a typical twenty-five to thirty years for a generation, it was computed that Ororoina was born in the last half of the seventeenth century. It was, furthermore, specifically computed that the great fire in *Ko te Umu o te Hanau Eepe*—the Long Ears' earth oven—occurred in the year 1680.

Although the legend of the Long Ears' fiery demise in the ditch was firmly believed by every native on Easter Island, the twentieth-century scientists who came to do investigative work felt that the legend was too improbable to be dignified by the classification of "history."

Some of them put forth the theory that the ditch had been dug at a far earlier date—to capture rainfall running off the Poike slopes for use in the irrigation of bananas. Others had equally unromantic observations to make—typified by the British geologist, L. J. Chubb, who claimed that the ditch had been created perhaps a million years ago by a flow of lava from the island's center which ran into an older hardened flow from Poike. The meeting of these two had caused the depression—and the natives of Easter later made up their legend to match the geographical peculiarity they found at the foot of Poike.

But Father Sebastian always persisted in his belief that the story of the most dramatic day in the island's history *was* history. He had no way, however, to prove his conviction until Thor Heyerdahl's archaeological expedition arrived on the island in 1955.

Until that time, no scientific methods of dating the past had ever been used on Easter Island. But by 1955, the technique of carbon-14 dating had been developed. All it required was the ashes of a fire. These ashes could be laboratory-tested for radio activity, and the date of the fire could thus be set, plus or minus a century or so.

The priest urgently requested Heyerdahl to set a team digging in Poike ditch where, if the legend held true, there would certainly be carbon for the carbon-14 datings.

Heyerdahl agreed, and the American archeologist Dr. Carlyle S. Smith, Professor of Anthropology at the University of Kansas, was put in charge of this dig.

To determine whether, in fact, there ever had been a fire in the ditch, Smith stationed six natives at widely separated spots along the grass-covered ditch which was visible only as a faint depression along the foot of the hillside. In some spots, the depression disappeared altogether. Each of the diggers was asked to make a six-foot-deep "test pit."

The men turned up nothing more than shovel after shovelful of fine yellow soil. But then there came a shout from the digger at Test Pit Number One. At a depth of two and a half feet, he had come across a strata of soil stained black with carbon of a fire. Below that lay a stripe of soft, reddish soil.

Then came a shout from the digger at Test Pit Number Two. Heyerdahl and Smith ran to Test Pit Two. Here, too, the digger had come to a broad black and red horizontal strip. The four other diggers found the same thing. It was indisputable. A great fire had once raged here in Poike Ditch!

They sent at once for Father Sebastian. When he arrived, he ran from hole to hole, looking down through the centuries. "His face," Heyerdahl reported, "was radiant."

The next morning, careful escavations began under Dr. Smith's directions.

It was found that the Poike Ditch did, in fact, follow the depression set by an ancient lava flow. But it was also found that men had dug their way down into the volcanic soil and rock and had made a defense ditch—twelve feet deep, some forty feet wide, and almost two miles long.

Carved stones, obsidian picks, and slingstones were buried deep in the volcanic ash. There were no bones, but this was not surprising. The bodies would have been thoroughly cremated in the blazing ditch.

The scientists and Father Sebastian were tremendously excited by what had been revealed. The natives, however, showed no surprise whatever. They had always known that this was *Ko te Umu o te Hanau Eepe*, the earth oven of the Hanau Eepe. They needed no diggings to reaffirm that fact.

But the final scientific amazement was to come.

Carbon samples were taken from the ditch. They were dried and immediately resealed for shipment to the laboratory when the expedition returned to the world from its navel.

In 1956, the samples were submitted to the *Nationalmuseets Mosselaboratorium* in Copenhagen for dating purposes.

Father Sebastian Englert, basing his computations on genealogy of the islanders, had previously put the date of the Poike Ditch fire at 1680. The scientists in Copenhagen, basing their computations on carbon-14 dating, and knowing nothing of island legends or genealogies, had put the year of the Poike Ditch fire at 1676.

Four years' difference!

Part III

The Modern Island and Discoveries of Easter's Most Ancient Past

chapter 9

In his report on the Poike Ditch digs, Dr. Carlyle S. Smith made a point which proved to be a vital one in the sharp separation of the golden age and the dark age which came after it.

> It is, perhaps, significant that no *mataa* [spearheads] were found in the excavations or on the surface, in view of the traditional association of this artifact with warfare, and the prevalence of the weapon, at least on the surface, at the majority of other sites.[1]

The Poike Ditch fire abruptly ended the era of the statue building, since it abruptly ended the men who were, presumably, the master statuemakers—the men who created long-eared moai in commemoration of their long-eared ancestors.

Yet, although a battle raged in and around the great ditch no sharp obsidian spearheads—*mataa*—were found there.

Obsidian had been used to make the statues. But not to make mataa. Indeed, the only weapons to turn up in Poike Ditch were a few sling stones. Slingshots were the most formidable armaments found as military relics of the golden age! What better indication could there be of the fact that peace reigned over the island during these creative halcyon years?

How *many* years? The islanders refer to the peaceable period which preceded the Long Ears–Short Ears War as *Karau-Karau*, which means "two hundred years."

They refer to the period after the Poike Ditch fire as *Huri-moai*, the Statue-overthrowing-Time.

Not only the statues were overthrown, but also almost every aspect of the remarkable culture which flourished before the Poike Ditch fire.

It is always easier to destroy than to create. And the moai were no exception. To see the giants crash to the ground, it was necessary only to dig a hole under the pedestals—and shove. Sometimes a huge slab of basalt was strategically set out in front of the statue so that when it toppled it would be beheaded, and therefore, could never be raised again.

Why were the moai overthrown? Perhaps, at first, because they reminded the Short Ears of their murdered long-eared enemies. Then, as the social structure swiftly, collapsed, *matatoa* (warriors) replaced *arikis* (chiefs) as leaders of local kin groups. And constant warring between kin groups replaced cooperation as the modus operandi of the island.

Each important kin group had its own standing statue which they revered as the representative of their tribe's ancient araki. It had always been believed that the head of an ariki, or chief, was the most sacred part of his body and the source of his mana, or supernatural powers. Mana enabled the chief to be middleman between his tribe and the gods.

So holy was the chief's head that his hair could never be cut. This policy persisted up until 1867 when little Gregario, the last *ariki mau*, lay dying of tuberculosis in the Catholic Mission. To make the lad more comfortable, one of the priests, Father Zumbohm, decided to cut the little prince's long tangled mat of hair. To his surprise, the boy protested wildly. But the priest persisted and an assistant who acted as barber began to cut. Gregario screamed for help. Islanders swarmed in, so angry that Father Zumbohm and the assistant were very nearly stoned. The islanders respected the priest, but far more important to them was the mana which lay in and around the head of the young ariki mau. When the boy died, many believed it was because of the haircut.

It becomes clear then why the warring tribes of the Statue-overthrowing-Time did their best to decapitate the towering stone image of a kin group's ancestor. Destroying the statue's supernatural powers was a shortcut to destroying the enemy tribe. (A statue thrown down with head intact retained its full quotient of mana.)

There was another popular method of destroying a tribe; the victors cooked and ate the vanquished, particularly the more tender women and children.

This had two virtues. There was not only a symbolic finality about the act of eating one's opponents, but—aside from rats —human flesh was the only source of red meat available on the island. Indeed, one of the chief attractions of these fighting forays was the prospect of the delectable feast which would be held at the end of it—the main item on the menu being the enemy.

Since tribal wars and cannibal feasts were held up until the time the three priests took up residence on the island, the details concerning this savage period do not depend on legends. They were vividly ingrained in the memories of old men and women who had witnessed or taken part in the wars. And they were duly recorded by the priests, by Alexander Salmon, who knew the native language; and by those for whom Salmon acted as interpreter and guide. As late as 1934, the noted ethnologist Alfred Métraux found natives who, as children, had known *hai-tangata:* man-eaters.

Every moai on the island was shoved from its ahu during the two-

century-long Statue overthrowing Time.

On the night before they went to war, the *matatoa* were not allowed to sleep. In any case, they may have been too busy to do so—there were many formalities in the prebattle ritual. Each warrior had to stain his entire body black. Then he sharpened his obsidian spearheads and hid any valuable items he might possess (a colorful crown of rooster feathers . . . a large gourd . . . a stone pillow . . . a red and yellow-painted tapa cloak). Finally, he ate a special meal prepared for him in a separate oven—by his father.

Women and children took part in the proceedings when dawn came. They followed the warriors to the scene of the battle, chanting to give the men courage, and reciting charms which hopefully might encourage the aku aku to turn against the enemy.

The onlookers retired to a hilltop to watch the battle and cheer on their side. There can be no doubt that their cheers were fervent, for if their men lost, the women and children could well end up in the stone-lined earth ovens.

The battle started traditionally with insults shouted back and forth between the contenders. The next stage was stone throwing. Then followed the hurling of obsidian-tipped spears.

After this, the warriors closed in for hand-to-hand combat. Some wielded long, wooden clubs with sharp edges. Some flailed about with short, flat clubs.

The mayhem continued until one side gave up and ran away—their women and children racing along with them. They often hid out in caves, which became traps when the victors discovered them and laid seige by posting warriors at the entrance. Meanwhile, other matatoa attacked the settlement of the defeated enemy, burned down the huts, destroyed the crops.

The final stage of the battle depended on just how angry the victors were. Sometimes, destruction of the settlement was deemed sufficient. Sometimes prisoners were taken off to work as farmhands—slaves in the fields of the victors. But if the battle was a serious one, so were the consequences. Victims were trampled on by the victors, until their guts spilled out. Others were hacked to pieces. Still others had their skulls broken. The lucky ones were merely tortured and then allowed to limp away, or were left to die on their own. More fortunate were the good-looking women and young girls. They were generally presented to victorious warriors as battle prizes.

The final climax of the proceedings was the cannibal feast. The *ika*—those to be eaten—were shut up in special huts in front of an ahu. Later, as the victors danced and chanted on the stone-cobbled plaza, the victims were slowly roasted in the umus. When this hot-stone cookery had been completed, the body was hacked up and the choicest parts given to the most important members of the victorious tribe. (Father Zumbohm was told that fingers and toes were considered a special delicacy.) Meat was served with side dishes which invariably included roast sweet potatoes.

If one of the victims happened to have been an ariki, he was accorded special treatment. After he was eaten, his skull was burned—to fully destroy his mana.

Further dancing and singing followed the feasts. These ceremonies were often performed by moonlight.

A German named Geiseler came to the island in 1882 and undertook an intensive four-day study for the Director of the Ethnographic Department of the *Kaiserliches Museum*. Salmon served as his interpreter and chief guide. Geiseler witnessed one of the moonlight dances which, he was told, had been performed after cannibal feasts. He described it thus:

> The dance differs from what is customary on other islands in Polynesia. . . . They stand here on one leg and stretch the

other while thrusting it out by jerks in the same rhythm as the song. . . . During the singing a carved figure representing a woman is usually moved by the leader of the choir, also on one leg in time with the dance.

The causes of the kin group wars ranged from the seemingly innocuous incident to the eminently understandable.

As an example of the former: A young boy who spied an eel asked a man on the beach to help him catch it. The man did so, and then took the eel off to his own hamlet's hara-hui (feasting hut) to be cooked. The boy followed him, complaining all the way. A large feast was being prepared in the hara-hui. The boy stayed, and when the eel was cooked, he was given only the tip of its tail to eat.

The lad went home and told his father what had happened. Without further ado, the irate father took up his club and stomped off to the feast site. People had eaten themselves into a stupor and lay sleeping. The father bashed the eel-stealer over the head, killed him and other sleeping tribesmen, and escaped.

This eel incident started a violent war which lasted for several years.

More comprehensible causes for tribal wars concerned the relatives of one who had been eaten. If the feaster remarked to a family member, "Your flesh has stuck between my teeth," this could arouse the insulted party to a rage which resulted in all-out tribal war. Another common insult was spitting the deceased's teeth in the face of one of his relatives.

Another cause of war came from the carefully kept "cousin taboo." Through all of their recorded history, the islanders seem to have had an inborn sense of eugenics. It was not permissible for first, second, or even third cousins to "cohabit."

One ardent young man named Taropa courted one of his cousins—or tried to. The girl would have nothing to do with him. So Taropa raped her. This started a tribal war—highlighted by the final fight between Taropa (who had been hiding out in a cave) and the girl's father (who found him there). The father stuck a bone dagger in Taropa's throat, and then drank the blood which gushed from the dead man's wound. He was not so much avenging his ravaged daughter, as the breaking of the cousin taboo, which defiled his entire family.

Because the island population was so small, and the cousin taboo so strict, infant betrothal was common—especially among the upper classes—chiefs, warriors, priests, the island version of witch doctors, and/or those who owned tracts of land. A baby bride-to-be would live with her future in-laws as their daughter. If, when she reached puberty, her fiancé refused to marry her, he had to placate the girl's parents by giving them gifts and a splendid feast.

Sometimes, the girl reached puberty when her betrothed was two years old. She then had to wait patiently for him to grow up.

The marriage ceremony was a simple affair, involving the exchange of food between the two families.

Divorce was also easy, requiring no formalities at all. And it could be caused by the simplest of spats. For example, the women and children of Easter Island could not partake of food until the man of the family had been served and had eaten his fill. If his fill meant that the scraps which were left did not suffice to fill the wife, and if she complained about the matter, this was cause for divorce—on her part, or his. And no one thought badly of either if they took up with another spouse.

Even a wife who stayed with the same man but presented

him with progeny sired by a variety of fathers was not frowned upon—as long as the third-cousin taboo was upheld.

Proudest of all was the wife who could present her husband with a child who had been fathered by a passing sailor. Indeed, the early visitors to Easter made surprised note of the fact that the island men seemed so anxious to see them respond to the unsubtle advances of the island girls that the men sometimes shoved the girls straight into a sailor's arms.

But there was—literally—more to this than met the eye. Captain Cook counted only fifty or so females on the island. Other visitors also noted the surprising absence of women. On the other hand, the female population came out full force for the friendly La Pérouse. It was clear, therefore, that the women hid from seamen who came ashore with firearms. Only those girls of a certain age and station were allowed out and encouraged to entice the sailors. Royal women and others who were highborn remained hiding in caves till the strangers had departed.

An island child who had been fathered by a foreigner was automatically set high in the island's status heirarchy. Indeed, in later years, the infant was often named after the ship which had brought the father. The mother did not always remember the name of the man, but each ship made an impression on island history. In fact, those few ships which arrived in the eighteenth and nineteenth centuries made such an impression that they figured in island legends, songs, dances, cave paintings, and rock carvings.

Small wonder that a child fathered from so heralded a ship woven into legends would, himself, become something of an island personage.

Small wonder, too, that even today the islanders reflect the world in their faces. Some have an Oriental tilt to the eyes. Others look as European as any so-called *Continentale*. There are pale-skinned redheads—who might have the genes of a red-headed sailor. But the redheads who show up in the Atan family insist that *their* hair coloring derives from their hallowed long-eared ancestor, Ororiana.

Many of today's islanders look purely Polynesian. But there are just as many who do not.

chapter 10

Although marriage was not celebrated with much of a ceremony by the post-Poike Ditch islanders, birth and death received their full due. The highlight of each such event was a feast.

The birth ceremony began when the woman was either three or five months pregnant. (These odd-numbered months were the lucky ones.) The in-laws all gathered for a ceremonial banquet. The mother-to-be was served only *umu-takapu-kokoma-moa*—chickens' guts roasted in an umu. The rest of the family fared far better, foodwise.

When the child came (a woman gave birth kneeling or squatting on the ground), anyone who happened to fancy the task cut the umbilical cord with his—or her—teeth. Then a priest was summoned to tie the newborn's cord in such a way as to make "a good navel"—one which stuck out prominently. This act tied in the infant's mana, which otherwise would have leaked out.

The elaborate ceremonial rites duplicated those described in such detail in the legends pertaining to the birth of Hotu Matua's first son when the founding father—and mother—arrived at Anakena.

The leftover umbilical cord was usually buried. That tiny

grave became a tapu spot. Anyone who who happened to walk on it was likely to get ulcers.

The father then gave a banquet for his maternal in-laws. Only certain foods were permitted at this particular feast. (Sweet potatoes were—for once—strictly excluded.)

When the baby was seven months old, it received a haircut (with an obsidian knife) from a paternal uncle. And it received a present—some chickens—from a maternal uncle. The child's first steps were rewarded with more chickens. Still more were presented when the legs of a male child were tattooed at the age of seven or eight. This, being a great event, was rewarded by thirty chickens—a present from a maternal uncle. These chickens were a giveaway gift. They could not be consumed by the child or his family. They were used to give away at other ceremonial functions.

Children seem to have had quite a pleasant life—when they did not become feast-meats at the end of a tribal war. They rode the surf on bundles of reeds, tied together. Sleds made of *ti* leaves were used to slide down the sides of a volcano. They flew kites—sticks covered by tapa cloth. They spun tops made of stone, clay, or nuts. And they played a lot of cat's cradle, embellished by the recitation of short poems.

Adolescents had their own "hangouts": secret caves or *hara-hui*—when the huts were not in use for the preparation of a feast. The pale-skinned youths made a special point of staying indoors, not wanting to spoil their beauty by becoming copper-toned in the sun.

And when they had nothing better to do, the youngsters played war. It was generally *Hotu-iti* versus *Tu'u,* which was not a mere matter of playacting teams like Cops and Robbers or Cowboys and Indians. The "teams" in this game were named after the two chief warring factions on the island.

Since the battle of Poike Ditch had finished off the Long

Ears—and most of the island culture as well, it might be assumed that the remaining islanders would be a bit wary about again dividing their tiny realm into two "sides." Yet, this is precisely what happened.

Every islander belonged to one of the ten mata, or tribes. The tribes who lived in the west and northwest sections were called the People of Tu'u; the easterners were called the People of Hotu-iti. In addition to battles which could break out at any time between any of the tribes or subtribes, there was a more or less everlasting state of war between the people of Tu'u and Hotu-iti.

When the women of the island were not involved in wars, they, too, seem to have led rather an easy life. They did the housework—which cannot have amounted to much since everyone lived either in a one-room reed hut (boat house), stone hut or cave. They made clothing—which also did not amount to much, since men wore only a loin cloth of beaten bark, and a tapa cloak for cool weather. Women wore the same, sometimes with the addition of a tapa mini-skirt.

And women did the cooking, again, which did not amount to much—except on feast days when the preparations were prodigious.

Women also helped to gather shellfish and harvest sweet potatoes and other crops. And during times of drought, they trudged along with the men to bring back water from the lakes which lay deep in the craters of the three large volcanoes.

The men were matato, warriors—which often involved a good deal of political power. Or they were *ivi atua*—"family of the gods," or priests. Or they were medicine men. If they were born lucky, they were ariki—of royal blood. They were given the first fruits, the best fish. And they were not expected to work.

Most of the men were *huru-manu* (the "commoners"):

fishermen, farmers, craftsmen. And lowest on the social scale
was the *kio*. A man who owned no land and worked for another as a sharecropper was called a kio. A kio was also one
who had been captured in a war and worked in the fields of
the victors. At night, these unfortunate kio-serfs were herded
into a cave under armed guard.

As is true in any society, life for the upper classes was en-
livened by parties. These were called *koro,* or festival-feast.
They were frequently given by a devoted son as a father's day
celebration.They were also given, on occasion, for a mother
—or even a mother-in-law.

Giving a koro was no simple matter on an island where
there was not much food to begin with, and where the food
supply which did exist was under constant peril of being
wiped out by tribal war. The food gathering required a good
bit of advance planning. A man had to cultivate extra fields
of crops in order to have sufficient food for the forthcoming
koro. If his crops were destroyed, he was forced to ask the
guests to help furnish supplies.

The biggest problem was chickens. It was necessary to have
three hundred of them: all alive and squawking.

In addition, the host had to hire a *hatu,* who composed special songs for the occasion. These were performed on feast
day by a special chorus of men and women. (The hatu was
paid for his services by an *umu*ful of food.)

Guests arrived, dressed in their finest. In addition to loin-
cloth and cape, this meant being bedecked in wooden ornaments hung around the neck. It also meant some kind of
headgear. The islanders had a passion for hats. There were
rooster-feather crowns. There were helmets made of woven
reeds, then covered with colored feathers. And women wore
woven-reed hats with wide brims and turned-up points at the
back.

Koro-giving continued into the twentieth century, when apparel included items traded with or stolen from visitors. Brother Eugène described koro garb like this:

> On their great days, they dress, adorn and load themselves with everything that can somehow be attached to them. The man who has been able to get hold of a dress puts on a dress; if he has two of them, he puts on two. The woman who can lay her hands on a pair of trousers, a waistcoat or an overcoat, decks herself out in them with all possible elegance.[1]

As for headgear, Brother Eugène noted that, in addition to feather crowns and reed hats, headgear was made of half a melon, a seabird whose carcass had been split open and cleaned out "more or less," a shoe, and two buckets set one inside the other.

With this intense interest in hats, it was small wonder that all early visitors to the island reported with some surprise that one's hat was almost impossible to keep on one's head. A moment of relaxation and he had been be-hatted by a native who snatched off the headgear and raced away with it.

Having arrived at the feast in all their finery, guests sat down to be entertained while food was taken from the ladened trestles and cooked in the *umus*. The same method of cooking was used, whatever the occasion. There was no pottery; there were no pots. The only utensil was the gourd to hold water. Therefore, nothing could be boiled. All cooking was done via hot stones in the stone-lined earth oven. A starting layer of stones was put in. When they grew very hot, they were removed from the pit, which was then lined with banana leaves, followed by a layer of food, more banana leaves, more hot stones. These layers built up until the top edge of the umu was reached, at which point there was a final covering of banana leaves, then earth. After a few hours, the food was dug up—steaming hot, juicy and delicious.

In addition to the ubiquitous yams, taros, and sweet potatoes, a traditional umuful of food contained spiny lobsters, eels, fish, and chickens.

However, the three hundred chickens at the koro were not eaten. They were tied together in groups of ten and then attached by the feet to a rope which had been strung between two sticks in the ground. Those chickens which had been brought as gifts by the guests were strung up the same way, on a rope which formed right angles to the first.

At the proper ceremonious moment, the host approached the *motuha*—the guest of honor—and gave him a chicken, which the motuha promptly passed on to a member of the family. The guest of honor then went up to the two strings of cackling chickens, and presented a cluster to his brother. The brother slung them onto his back, where the fowl—still tied together by their feet—formed a kind of squawking cape which provided noisy accompaniment as the brother did an improvised dance.

When the motuha's brother had finished prancing about, the guest of honor untied all the chickens and presented them to other relatives. Each chicken was at once passed on to someone else—for the rule was that a fowl could not be eaten until it had been given to five different guests.

The chicken gifts were taken home by the various guests. And the host, happily, usually ended up with a number of fowl to replace his own supply of chickens which had often been depleted to the point of extinction by the preparations for the party.

After all the chicken exchanging, the umus were opened and the feasting started.

As the guests stuffed themselves, the chorus performed.

The singers and dancers were generally the adolescent boys and girls who rehearsed for weeks before the event in the empty feast huts. (Along with the rehearsing—in the carefully chosen words of ethnologist Métraux, "the youngsters made their first acquaintance with the delights of love.")

When they performed, the chorus was often divided into a row of *pere* (men) and another row of *ihi* (women) under the direction of the hatu, the composer of the ceremonial song. First the pere would sing a verse, then the ihi, while the hatu stood between them keeping time with an *oa* (a ceremonial paddle).

Early visitors who witnessed such singing were struck by the range of voices, from deep bass to highest falsetto. The women knelt, swayed, and moved their hands as they sang. Pierre Loti described a performance he witnessed in 1872:

> They all sing beating their hands as if they were making a dance rhythm. The women utter notes soft and fluty as those of birds. The men sometimes make small falsetto voices, thin, quavering, and shrill. Sometimes, they produce cavernous sounds like the roars of enraged wild animals. Their music is made of short and jerky phrases, ending in gloomy vocalizations descending in minor tones. They seem to express the surprise of being alive and also the sadness of life.[2]

The host invariably got his money's worth (or his umu's worth) from the hatu who composed the ceremonial song—for the song went on, and on. There was endless repetition, and minute attention to details. For example, the natives had named virtually every coastal indentation, every hillock, even large boulders on the island. If a song involved the guest of honor making a trip to visit his son who lived with another kin group, the names of the rocks, hillocks, and inlets he passed were mentioned in the hatu's song. And then when the hero returned home, the same rocks, hillocks, and inlets were mentioned once more.

Singing was usually accompanied by dancing—often the one-footed, hopping variety, in which the other leg was jerked in rhythm to the song. The dancers did no leaping or twirling. Their movements were graceful and slow.

Musical accompaniment was provided by the clacking together of seashells.

The most impressive kind of koro was the *paina*—or funeral feast. The songs composed for such an occasion were suitably gloomy. One of them went:

E hata tae kava	The stinking worms
E kaikai koe	Eat you,
ai Tau-mahani	O Tau-mahani,
I te vie honui e.	Woman of high lineage.

A paina was generally held several years after the person had died, and unless the deceased was truly "a woman of high lineage," painas were usually organized only for a man of the family.

A replica of the dead man was made: reeds and sticks covered by a "skin" of bark. Hair was made by reeds; eyes by discs cut from a skull. Pupils were black shells, and eyebrows were formed by feathers. The bark was then painted with black designs to represent tattooing. These effigies stood from nine to twelve feet tall. They were placed by an ahu, and then framed by a circle of stones.

Both González, head of the Spanish expedition, and La Pérouse witnessed paina ceremonies in the eighteenth century. They described how the organizer of the ceremony (usually a son or brother of the deceased) first surrounded the effigy with food(including the inevitable sweet potatoes and chickens).

Then the host climbed inside and made a glowing speech which extolled both the dead man and his own generosity in giving this feast. He addressed the gathering through a hole which represented the effigy's mouth.

The crowd responded by weeping and loud laments. This was cut short at the proper time by the orator, who stuck his hand out of the effigy's mouth—holding a live rooster at arm's length. When silence fell, he stepped out of the circle of stones and distributed the food.

Not every dead man was fortunate enough to receive a proper piana. But most received some sort of funeral, which ranged from elaborate to casual.

In the latter variety, the corpse was wrapped in a mat of reeds and left to rot in front of an ahu. After two or three years, the sun-bleached bones were strewn on the ahu or stuck in between its stones.

The more elaborate funerals involved—of course—a feast. Food for the immediate family of the deceased was prepared in a *umu papaku* (dead man's oven). Distant relatives and friends cooked their own food in separate small ovens. The "master of the corpse"—the closest relative of the deceased, handed out this food. But *his* food had to be cooked in still another oven. If he did not abide by this important rule, he would die within the year.

While the funeral meats were cooking, there came a specially composed funeral lament. If no other theme could be thought of, there was always that old standby: food. One typical lament:

> *Alas, alas what will become of us?*
> *Alas for us, father, O father who brought much food,*
> *Many fish, many yams, many sweet potatoes,*
> *Many eels, much sugar cane, many bananas.*
> *O father, great fisherman, your taut line sung.*
> *Alas, alas, what will become of us?*

During the time of the cannibals, those bodies which were not cooked in earth ovens were left to rot on, or by, an ancient ahu, or altar. Bones were then hidden between the ahu stones.

Nor was the food theme dropped after the funeral, for the dead man's soul hovered about for a time begging food from the living. Finally, unless it had some special reason for remaining (revenge, improper burial), it flew off into the *Po* (the night) where ancestors came in boats to meet the new arrival. He kept the same status he had had on earth, and lived much the same sort of life.

There was one contingency, however, which kept a man or woman from being buried according to form, no matter how important a personage the deceased may have been. If he—or she—had been cooked and eaten, bones and teeth were strewn about with abandon. Human bones, including skulls, can still be found all over the island, particularly in caves where cannibal feasts were often held. One spacious cave, particularly popular for this purpose, was decorated with beautiful rock paintings of boats and birds. The place is called *Ana Kai Tangata* which means "Cave Where Men Are Eaten."

chapter 11

It is generally accepted that the dark and destructive period, when the island was ruled by warriors and cannibals, lasted from the time of the Poike Ditch fire in 1680 until the French priests settled in for several years in the 1860s—almost two centuries.

Coincidentally, according to the name the natives gave to their golden age Karau-Karau—Two Hundred Years—the zenith and the depths of this Stone Age civilization lasted about the same span of time.

The savagery and cannibalism would not, perhaps, seem quite so stark had it not directly followed the astounding civilization achieved by the statuemakers, and had that civilization not been totally destroyed.

There were, however, some very special elements in the Statue-making period which survived well into the Statue-overthrowing-Time. One of these was the reading of the rongorongo tablets.

Though the massive moai have brought world renown to this tiny island, many experts believe that even more remarkable are the small wooden tablets inscribed with hundreds of tiny symbols and figures, exquisitely cut out in neat rows of mysterious writing: *ko hau motu mo rongorongo:* "lines of script for recitation."

In his last book, *Island in the Center of the World,* Father Sebastian wrote:

> Though their meaning remains unknown to us, the tablets themselves still stand as a unique monument to the cultural sophistication of this tiny and isolated community that is far more important than the largest of the stone statues at Rano Raraku. . . .
>
> Written languages, wherever found, are almost always the product of large societies and complicated cultures which have great masses of information that require recording. They result from this need and are indeed unusual as products of small and isolated groups. That a script would be needed or invented by the tiny community of Easter Island is genuinely astonishing. Yet no source away from the island from which this script could have been derived has yet been identified.

Not all language experts agree with Father Sebastian's statement that the script is unrelated to any source away from the island. Even the legends state that the writing was brought to the island by the great king Hotu Matua. Indeed, the legends are most specific about the matter.

The king brought with him from Hiva sixty-seven inscribed tablets. In addition, he brought *maori ko hau rongorongo*— masters who knew the art of writing and reciting the tablets.

The tablets—according to ancient traditions—fell into four categories. There were hymns in honor of Make-Make and other gods *(ko hau kiri take ki te atua)*. There were tablets which recorded crimes of men *(ho hau ta'u)*. There were tablets which recorded the deeds of those who fell in wars *(ko hau ika)*. And it is said that there were also tablets bearing genealogical records. Nothing more is known about these, though historically, they might have been the most valuable of all.

Legend certainly moves into reality when it comes to the

matter of the rongorongo schools. Legend has it that the wooden tablets were under the direct supervision of the ariki henua, first Hotu Matua, and then the kings who descended from him.

Hotu Matua organized the first school to teach the art of writing and reading the tablets. The maori ko hau rongorongo who had come with him in the double canoe were the first teachers. But the schools obviously went on through the centuries—until the tragic day of the Peruvian slave raid in 1862. As it happened, every native who knew how to read the rongorongo tablets was captured. And every one of them died.

There did, however, remain on the island a few who had attended the rongorongo school. Though they did not remember what they had learned, they remembered details about the school.

In 1886, Paymaster Thomson met an old man named Ure Vaeiko who had studied in one of the schools as a boy. In 1914, Mrs. Scoresby-Routledge interviewed an old man named Te Haha, and another, a leper named Tomenika—both of whom had gone to the rongorongo school. In 1934, Métraux interviewed the nephew of Te Haha, who remembered his uncle's stories of the rongorongo school days. And as late as the 1940s, Father Sebastian met several islanders who had known an old man who—in his youth—had attended one of the schools near Ahu Akapu on the west coast.

Every effort was made to jog the memories of these one-time rongorongo students. Paymaster Thomson was able to buy two of the rongorongo boards (which he later gave to the National Museum in Washington D.C. and are now priceless). He was determined to have his tablets read. He located Ure Vaeiko who "professes to have been under instruction in the art of hieroglyphic reading at the time of the Peruvian visit, and claims to understand most of the characters."

However, Ure had become a good Catholic and believed that revealing what the tablets said might endanger his eternal salvation for the rongorongo were remnants of paganism. In the paymaster's words:

> He declined to furnish any information, on the ground that it had been forbidden by the priests. Presents of money and valuables were sent him from time to time, but he invariably replied to all overtures that he was now old and feeble and had but a short time to live, and declined most positively to ruin his chances for salvation by doing what his Christian instructors had forbidden.
>
> Finally the old fellow, to avoid temptation, took to the hills with the determination to remain in hiding until after the departure of the *Mohican.* It was a matter of the utmost importance that the subject should be thoroughly investigated before leaving the island, and unscrupulous strategy was the only resource after fair means had failed.

The paymaster's "unscrupulous strategy" does not seem all that evil. Thomson and his interpreter-guide, Salmon, set out in a veavy storm to Mataveri, where Uru lived. They reasoned that the old man would come in out of the rain and seek the shelter of his hut. And indeed, they found him there. The paymaster had come on his quest armed with a bottle of "the cup that cheers," plus photographs he had made in Tahiti of the rongorongo tablets owned by Bishop Jaussen.

First, Uru was asked to relate some island legends, which he seemed pleased to do. Then, as Thomson put it:

> During the recital certain stimulants that had been provided for such an emergency were produced and, though not pressed upon our ancient friend, were kept prominently before him until, as the night grew old and the narrator weary, he was included as "the cup that cheers" made its occasional rounds.

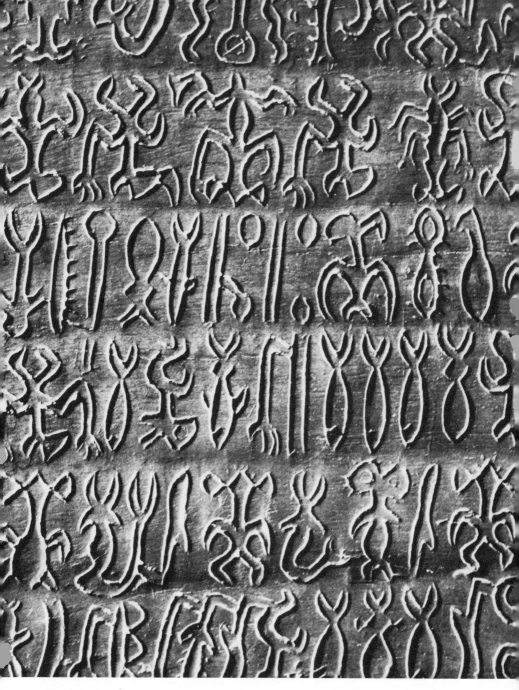

Detail of a wooden rongorongo board with the only known writing ever developed in Polynesia. The strange and beautiful hieroglyphics pose another of Easter's mysteries. Scholars have struggled unsuccessfully to read the rongorongo writing.

A judicious indulgence in present comforts dispelled all fears in regard to the future state, and at an auspicious moment the photographs of the tablets owned by the bishop were produced for inspection. Old Ure Vaeiko had never seen a photograph before, and was surprised to find how faithfully they reproduced the tablets which he had known in his young days. A tablet would have met with opposition, but no objection could be urged against a photograph, especially something possessed by the good bishop, whom he had been instructed to reverence.

Although Ure chanted on fluently:

> . . . it became obvious that he was not reading the characters. When the photograph of another tablet was substituted, the same story was continued without the change being discovered. The old fellow was quite discomposed when charged with fraud at the close of the all-night session. . . . He explained at great length that the actual value and significance of the symbols had been forgotten, but the tablets were recognized by unmistakable features . . . just as a person might recognize a book in a foreign language and be perfectly sure of the contents without being able to actually read it.[1]

Bishop Jaussen in Tahiti had an opposite experience when he found a native of Easter, called Metoro, who claimed to be able to read the rongorongo tablets. Metoro was shown the same tablet on three different days—and recited an entirely different legend each day.

As Father Sebastian summed it up, "Similar results were obtained by others who consulted islanders with reputations as *maori ko hau rongorongo*. It appears that by this time the last of the truly literate *maori* were dead."[2]

However, at least all the sources consulted agreed on what happened in the rongorongo schools.

The teachers were noblemen and often related to the king.

And the students were generally sons or nephews of the teachers.

Schools were held in special huts. When students showed up in the morning, they answered their teacher's welcoming greeting with their own cheerful chorus: *"Ko koe a."* Each student had a flat stone as a desk and a frigate bird's bone as a pen. An assistant teacher called the role to see that no one was playing hooky.

Sometimes, the king himself came along to visit the school. One ariki heuna, King Nga'ara, was particularly remembered for his keen interest in rongorongo. When visiting, he would often recite a long poem, swaying from side to side as he did so. He felt that the yearly examinations were very important. But if a student failed the test, the king blamed only the teacher. (When the scholarly King Nga'ara died, he was carried to his ahu on a bier made of rongorongo boards—which were buried with him.)

During the student's first years at the school, he was taught a number of chants which he performed while playing "cat's cradle." Some of these chants were spells to be recited in case of danger. Some helped crops to grow. Some concerned death, life, and love.

When the student's memory was well honed, he was started on the rongorongo writing. First, he made signs on banana leaves, for wood was too rare to waste on beginners.

Once a year, the king sponsored a competition at Anakena in which students, teachers, families, and friends gathered to hear the masters of rongorongo recite. This festival was generally regarded as so important that even if a war happened to be raging on the island, a truce was called until the annual competition (and the feast which followed) was over.

Only twenty-four rongorongo boards have survived. They are found in museums in Chile, the United States, and Europe.

Most are kept in cellar vaults, with only their plastic replicas on view. Some are in a sad state of decay. One was partly burned. But some seem as clear as the day they were made.

The wooden boards range from twelve to twenty inches in length and are covered on both sides by neat lines of tiny figures engraved into the wood. Some look like stylized animals or humans. All figures are the same size; a fish hook is as tall as a man.

Although none of the natives interviewed about rongorongo knew what the writing said, most knew how it was read. The reader starts at the left, on the lowest line. Upon reaching the end of that line, the tablet is turned upside down and the next line is read. The letters follow each other in snakelike formation. At the top of the tablet, the reading continues at the top line on the other side, and "snakes on" down.

Father Sebastian was just one of the language experts who spent countless hours trying to interpret the writing. He described it thus:

> . . . beautifully incised symbols, each generally from ⅜ to ⅝ of an inch long. The symbols include a fascinating multitude of little figures of men in a variety of positions, flying birds, animals, what appear to be plants, celestial objects, and geometrical forms. They are complex in detail yet at the same time drawn with calligraphic flow. There are hundreds of different signs—far too many to suggest any sort of phonetic alphabet or syllabary. The sequence of the writing is a rare and curious one called "reversed boustrophedon." . . . There is no doubt that this writing was inscribed by experts and that it represents a work of art as well as a script.[1]

Unfortunately, Brother Eugène, the first outsider to set eyes on the rongorongo boards, was not as impressed by the writing as was Father Sebastian. In his very first letter from the island, he reported having seen in all the native huts tablets and staves covered with strange signs. He added that the natives seemed to attach no particular importance to them. Nor, obviously, did Brother Eugène.

In 1886, William Thomson wrote the following in relation to the fact that of the thousands of rongorongo boards seen by Brother Eugène in 1864, only a few could be found by the paymaster:

> In explanation of the disappearance of these tablets, the natives stated that the missionaries had ordered all that could be found to be burned, with a view to destroying the ancient records, and getting rid of everything that would have a tendency to attach them to their heathenism, and prevent their thorough conversion to Christianity. The loss to the science of philology by this destruction of valuable relics is too great to be estimated.[2]

As late as 1954, Thor Heyerdahl was told by the natives that when Brother Eugène introduced Christianity to the island, he had put a taboo upon the hieroglyphic boards "so that all who touched them should die." This, writes Heyerdahl in *Aku Aku,* "the natives fully and firmly believed."

Father Sebastian gave three reasons for the disappearance of all the rongorongo boards except for those two dozen which had been rescued by visitors to the island.

1. Many houses were burned during the island wars, and the tablets in the houses naturally burned, too.

2. Many of the sacred tablets were kept by the islanders in secret caves, and they decomposed in the underground dampness.

3. The islanders feared that the aku aku—magic spirits— would be angry if the rongorongo tablets were sold to foreigners and taken from the island. The spirits would inflict dire vengeance on the man who so much as revealed the whereabouts of a rongorongo board.

Whatever the reasons for their disappearance, disappear they did in the space of the two decades between Brother Eugène's casual comment about the tablets and Paymaster Thomson's persistant search to learn their mysteries.

Another man who recognized the uniqueness of this hieroglyphic writing was Bishop Jaussen in Tahiti.

Father Gaspard Zumbohm, one of the priests on Easter Island, fell ill and returned to Tahiti. Among the interesting native "souvenirs" the sick priest showed to his bishop was a rongorongo tablet to which a cord of braided human hair was attached.

The bishop became tremendously excited. Then an Easter Island native who had accompanied the priest to Tahiti casually mentioned that the tablets were now being used by his people for lighting fires in the earth ovens. Upon hearing this, Bishop Jaussen sent word at once to Father Roussel, who still remained on Easter, ordering the priest to collect every rongorongo board he could find.

Roussel did so. But he could find only five—all of which he sent on to the Bishop. It proved to be the largest collection of rongorongo boards ever made.

This scarcity of samples was, of course, no help to the scholars who have tried to decipher the writing. But it has not deterred them.

The first to set the philological world humming on the subject of rongorongo was a Hungarian linguist named Guillaume de Hévesy who presented a lengthy paper to the *Académie des Inscriptions et Belles Lettres* in 1932. He had discovered similarities between some one hundred Easter Island hieroglyphs and a still undeciphered script which had recently been discovered in the Indus Valley. At first, there was great excitement. Had Hotu Matua come from India?

But the excitement waned when other scholars pointed out that this Indus Valley civilization predated Easter's by at least 1,000 years, and also that some 13,000 miles separated Easter from the banks of the Indus. Furthermore, aside from those one hundred or so hieroglyphs, the two civilizations had virtually nothing in common.

In 1398, a Viennese scholar, Robert von Heine-Geldern, published a monograph in which he pointed out that some ten hieroglyphs found on the rongorongo tablets not only had strong similarities to those found in the Indus Valley—but also to symbols found in ancient Chinese.

In 1958, another German, Thomas Barthel, Professor of Ethnology at the University of Tubingen, published a master work which included detailed descriptions of all the rongorongo boards in existence, plus the texts of the various chants made by Metoro for Bishop Jaussen, plus his own scholarly commentary on the objects represented in each of the hieroglyphs.

Father Sebastian summed up the general reaction to the most controversial part of "this voluminous work. . . . The translations it provides are not very intelligible."

Other scholars spent years studying the problem: three Russians, an Argentinian, and a Swiss professor named von Koenigswald. Each had his theories—and his followers—but none was hailed as having found the answer.

In his book *Easter Island: A Stone Age Civilization in the Pacific* Alfred Métraux pointed out:

> When we are endeavouring to decipher an unknown script, the first thing to do is to classify and count the signs. This I have tried to do with the tablet known as Aruku-kurenga. Out of a total of 960 symbols, the image of the sooty tern— symbolizing the god Make-Make—is repeated 183 times. Nearly a fifth of the tablet is, therefore, covered by a single

sign. An individual with a lozenge for a head is reproduced 94 times. Depictions of human beings and birds represent about one-third of the symbols. This proportion does not seem to favour the hypothesis of a syllabic or alphabetic script.

Métraux put forth the idea that each hieroglyph represented a whole line of a chant, or even a whole verse. It acted merely as a cue, or a clue. "To read the tablet the bard would have to know the text of the chant by heart, and the sole purpose would be to save him from lapses of memory that would be considered very bad omens."

Father Sebastian pointed out another difficulty in translating the tablets:

> . . . the script represented archaic forms no longer used, the language of old poetry, and obscure allusions to things, ideas and events now unknown, which must have been abundant in the literature of the tablets. To obtain insights of this kind it would be necessary to call back from their tombs the long-dead *maori* [masters]. The speech of the modern islanders, while still a Polynesian language, has undergone considerable evolution and has received many loan words from Tahitian, Spanish, English, and other languages. It is very different from the language in which the script must have been written.[3]

Perhaps the best summation of rongorongo reading was put forth by Father Sebastian in a single sentence: "That the *ko hau rongorongo* will ever be deciphered seems unlikely."

chapter 12

There were other elements which carried over from the golden age of the Stone Age islanders through the two centuries of darkness and destruction.

One of these was the painful practice of tattooing. The fact that this was a carry-over became clear when archaeologists with the Heyerdahl expedition dug down below the massive heads of several of the stone giants at the base of Rano Raraku and revealed pristine stone bodies.

These statues had been set in deep holes by the statue-makers themselves, as a way of propping up the stone men while the finishing touches were pecked into the backs. Unlike all the other statues on the island, these giants had not been exposed to centuries of pocking by wind-blown sand. Their excavated bodies were notably lighter in color than the weather-burnished brown faces which sat above the soil. And the careful body carvings were as clear as the day they had been completed.

In addition to such details as long fingernails and a large round navel, there were intricate designs which could only have represented tattooing. Indeed, some of the same tattoos were used in the Statue-overthrowing-Time, particularly the spirals, circles, and other geometrical designs. There were also a few boats, which perhaps were permanent memories of an historic or legendary event. In later years, too, historic happenings occasionally received this type of pricked-out permanence. For example, the captain on Pierre Loti's ship had ordered his sailors to carry off a statue. This event was recorded on the tattooed arm of a native.

From Roggoveen in 1722 through Brother Eugène in 1864, visitors had been impressed by the elaborate tattooing on many of the island men.

The tattooing process generally started when a boy was eight. The tattooist worked with a small comblike instrument made of bird bone. The prongs were dipped in a pigment made from ti stems mixed with poporo juice. Then the tattooist tapped the comb with a mallet to drive it into the skin.

The women generally favored body painting. And no wonder.

Tattooing was so painful a business that some men could not endure it—and went about all their lives with a half-finished motif testifying to their cowardice.

A man's bravery, as well as his affluence, could be ascertained by a quick onceover of his body. Many men had thighs and legs so thoroughly tattooed, they looked as though they were wearing breeches. The back, of course, provided a fine area for the tattooist's pricking. And, as Roggoveen had noted, "wonderful birds and animals" frequently covered a man's entire body.

Some went even further. Their necks were tattooed, their faces, and many islanders had the mucous membrane of the lips tattooed—often with alternating bands of colors.

Many of the moai have furrows around the mouth and neck, with curved lines from ear to ear sloping straplike under the jaw. This undoubtedly represented tattooing.

Another holdover which, according to legend, dates from Hotu Matua's day, was the kin group or tribal system of social organization. Indeed, as late as 1955 Métraux reported: "If any inhabitant of Hanga-roa village is asked the name of his tribe, he will unhesitatingly reply Marama, Tapa-hotu, Nga-ure or Miru, as the case may be."[1]

Miru has always been a prestigious tribe, since its descendants reputedly date back to Miru, the second son of Hotu Matua to whom the great king bequeathed the land from Anakena to Hanga-roa.

Still another holdover from prehistoric days are the aku akus—who are particularly operative in the nighttime. With the exception of Make-Make, who has always been the chief god on Easter Island, the other major dieties of the early days are remembered, if at all; in the names of ahus and certain island sites. But the second-class spirits—the aku aku—lost little of their potency through the passage of time. Although Christianity may have laid the major gods to rest, it affected the aku aku in one way only: Some devout Catholics came to call them *tatane,* the island version of the word "Satan." But the aku aku were not all satanic. Some were kindly and often brought gifts to one of their pet persons: a turtle, a piece of driftwood, a stray chicken.

Others were spooky. One long-armed lady aku aku would stand in the sea and scoop a solitary climber off a cliff in the nighttime. And there were numerous cannibal ghosts who came at night to demand food: They particularly fancied human intestines.

There were Robin Hood types who stood waiting in the darkness when food was being cooked at night in an earth oven. Then they summoned the head of the household to demand food—not for themselves but for hungry humans (living ones).

Most of the aku aku ranged from mischievous to evil. The spirits could take any form. They could enter a human, a bird, a turtle. They could perform mild pranks such as giving a man a nosebleed. Other pranks had more serious consequences. A favored pastime of aku akus—shoving someone off a cliff at night.

Many of them lived in specific places and were known to the natives by name. In 1914, Mrs. Scoresby-Routledge made a list of some ninety aku akus with their names and their island addresses. Many of these names are forgotten by now. But it is still hard to find a native Pascuense who will declare with certainty that aku akus do not roam the island in the nighttime. Many claim they have seen aku akus or heard one speak in its thin, shrill voice.

There were other evil spirits—those which specialized in punishing people by making them ill. However, any sick islander had an ally: the medicine man, who often doubled as a pagan priest.

If someone fell ill, the medicine man was sent for at once. Instead of inquiring as to the patient's aches and pains, he demanded to know what *tapu* (taboo) the suffering one had violated. Had he, perhaps, eaten fish during the winter months, when such a deed was (for no known reason) tapu and would mean certain death? Or did he, perhaps, have an enemy who had caused evil to enter the sick man's body by burying a rooster head down in a hole and then jumping on the spot where the bird was dying of suffocation? (This was the prime time for pronouncing a curse on one's enemy: usually, a wish that he be stricken with some evil spirit which would cause his quick demise.)

If the patient was innocent of any tapu he might have violated—or knew of no enemy who might wish him harm—the medicine man entered the second stage of treatment: He ignored the sick person and turned his attention to the evil spirit lurking inside. In a kindly voice, he invited the spirit "out." But if the evil spirit turned deaf ears to such gentle means, the medicine man closed the door of the hut, sometimes even placed a net over the entire hut to catch the spirit when it did try to leave. Then the medicine man proceeded to jump, shriek, shout, and perform frightening incantations. If the spirit shot out of the sick person's body, the medicine man sprang against the walls to catch it, jump on it, and, hopefully, strangle it.

As the final stage of treatment, the medicine man took the sick person's clothes and other belongings and threw them into a fire which had been lit nearby. When all had burned, he smilingly returned and told the patient that he or she was now completely cured.

If, despite all these energetic ministrations, the patient remained as ill as ever, the medicine man answered with a sad shrug. Although the first evil spirit had been driven out, an even more evil one had obviously taken over where the first left off.

Some particularly diligent practitioners would then try a few further steps—simple massage followed by an all-over sweat which was induced by digging a coffin-length umu, covering the white-hot stones with a mattress of banana leaves and putting the patient in the hot spot for a while.

Not everyone, of course, could afford the services of a medicine man for, like doctors anywhere, their fees were high. They usually charged in chickens. If their fees were not met, the revenge of the medicine man could be as terrible as that of the evil spirit which had entered the patient's body in the first place. And, as with all doctors, fees had to be paid whether or not the cure had been effected.

Easter Island's longest and most elaborate religious festival also lasted throughout the nineteenth century. This was the great Birdman Festival. As late as 1938, Alfred Métraux interviewed a native named Tepano, whose uncle had been one of the last birdmen—and had never tired of talking about it. The French priests wrote detailed descriptions of the festival, as did other nineteenth-century visitors to the island.

The months-long drama was certainly unique.

The setting was the amazingly round Rano Kau volcano in the Southwestern corner of the island triangle. Pierre Loti described the crater thus:

> . . . possibly the most regularly shaped in the entire world. . . . It is an immense colosseum where you could easily maneuver a great army. . . . The footpaths are full of bones and whole skeletons still appear half lost in the grass.[2]

In the center of the steep-walled crater lies a lake, a half mile wide, which is carpeted by a mat of green bog and totora reeds. And high on the rearing western lip of the crater, scattered along the precipice for some 800 feet, are some fifty specially built, partly subterranean, stone houses, used only at the time of the Birdman Festival.

Even when no festival proceedings are in progress, this site has its own built-in drama. Behind the stone houses is the sheer cliff drop to the green lake, and at the front door, the cliff falls straight down some 1,000 feet to the ocean, where waves crash with the sound of eternity against jutting black rocks and white sea spray lurches high into the air.

Within swimming distance lie three tiny islets, which jut abruptly from the sea, and they, too, play a part in the proceedings.

The ceremonies began each July at the foot of Rano Kau. The place was called Mataveri and here the VIPs of the island gathered: warriors, princes, priests, some of the rongorongo teachers, and other kin group dignitaries. They lived in large ceremonial huts while they rehearsed their dances and prepared their costumes.

Then, faces painted black and red, heads adorned with feather crowns, the participants danced, shouted, and chanted their way up the footpath to the clifftop heights, all the while waving their dance paddles or *ao* in the air. (This path is still called The Way of the *Ao*.)

When they reached Orongo, they settled into the stone houses to watch and wait. And every islander on Easter waited, too, caught in the grip of the excitement. *Who would be the next Birdman of the Year?*

The candidates were the chief warriors of each important kin group. Every man who put himself up for the title had selected a *hopu*—a servant. While the masters were busy dancing, feasting and decorating themselves at Mataveri, these servants had to paddle through shark-infested waters from the foot of the Rano Kau cliff to one of the three islets: Motu Nui. There the servants sat waiting to see who would be the first to spot the first egg laid by the returning sooty terns, who used the islet as their winter resort. Sometimes this watching took weeks. The hopu brought food with them in their reed canoes. They lived in caves on the tiny island. But aside from snatches of sleep, and snacks of sweet potatoes, bananas, and such, the servants did nothing whatever but watch for that all-precious speckled first egg.

The lucky hopu who spotted it would snatch up the egg, leap onto a high rock, and cry out the name of his master; this was followed by the directive: "Shave your head!"

Then the hopu dipped the holy egg into the sea, bound it to his forehead, plunged into the water, and started frantically to swim toward shore.

If he were not chewed up by sharks, and if he was able to

At the height of the Birdman of the Year contest, the island's chief warriors waited on the cliff-top heights of Orongo, where rocks had been carved with petroglyphs of birdmen. The hopu—or servant—of each warrior waited on Moto Nui, largest of the three tiny islets. The hopu who spotted the first egg laid by a sooty tern had to swim back with it through shark-infested waters and deliver it to his master—who thus became the Birdman of the Year.

clamber up the sheer cliff to Orongo, and if the precious egg had not been broken through all of this activity, the hopu handed the egg to his master—who thus became the new Birdman of the Year. He was the Chosen One—chosen by none other than the great god Make-Make himself.

The new birdman shaved his head, his eyebrows, his eyelashes. A priest tied a piece of holy tapa cloth around the holy arm which had received the holy egg. Then the new birdman, with a big wooden bird tied to his back, and the precious egg in the palm of his hand, led an exalted procession down the path. Trembling, jerking, he shrilled a chant in a birdlike voice.

As Tepano described the scene to Métraux:

> The men leapt about, twirling their dance paddles. They wore wigs made of women's hair. Others wore turbans of tapa or garlands of leaves. They brandished their paddles and made their bodies tremble.[3]

At Mateveri, the celebrants stopped for a feast. Human victims—preselected by priests—were roasted in the umus and, when done to a turn, were eaten by the excited kinfolk of the new birdman. The disappointed relatives of all the other would-be birdman started fights at the banquet; some ballooned into tribal wars which lasted for months.

The birdman was, perhaps, sorry to see the banquet come to a close, for afterward, he had to retire to a holy hut where he lived all alone for a year. Not only was he forbidden to emerge from his dwelling, but he could not take a bath for a year, and he spoke to no one except a special manservant who cooked his food. If, by any chance, a woman was seen entering the hut, the sacred birdman was immediately put to death.

The birdman took a new name—which became the Name of the Year. For instance, the year 1866–67 was the Year of Rokunga, the name adopted by Tepano's uncle when he became birdman.

There are no more birdmen on Easter Island, but the visitor who climbs to the cliff-top edge of Rano Kau feels their presence. For the ancient witnesses to the strange ceremonies are still there: Carved into the rocks at Orongo are the petroglyphs of the great Make-Make and the bird-headed symbols of the men who had been chosen as the living representatives of Easter Island's most powerful god.

chapter 13

For the first half of the twentieth century, Easter Island was, in effect, a vast sheep farm. The British company that leased the land from Chile made a handsome profit from its 40,000 sheep which produced 150,000 pounds of annual wool. But Messrs Williamson, Balfour & Co. paid little attention to the human population of the island.

In fact, the human population was not their responsibility. As Mr. Smith, the Scottish manager of the company, put it to Alfred Métraux in 1934, "Chile doesn't care about the natives —she takes absolutely no interest in them. We try to stick loyally to our undertakings; we try to be humane; and the result is we are accused of the very abuses we do our best to avoid."[1]

Métraux had heard much of these abuses, for he had spent some time in Chile where he was regaled with tales of the brutal British who had shut off the natives into a corner of the island and refused them the right to wander freely on the 45,000 square acres which comprised their small land. He had heard that the British company shamefully underpaid its native workers; that they shamefully overcharged the islanders for goods bought at the company store.

When Métraux put forth these points, he was told by an

indignant Mr. Smith that, in fact, the company paid its native workers more than those in Chile received for the same type of jobs.

Furthermore, the goods sold in the company store were at wholesale prices, irrespective of the cost of transporting the merchandise some 3,250 miles from Chile. Indeed, the values in the store were so good that Chilean sailors shopped there during shore leave—creating another problem, since the store was chronically low on every sort of item. (The Chilean supply ship visited Easter only once a year.)

As to the charge of confining the natives to a corner of their island, Smith explained that if the natives were not so prone to purloining the company's sheep, the barbed wire fence surrounding the village would not be necessary. Even with the fence and the special passes issued to anyone wanting to cross the island after sunset, some 3,000 sheep managed to vanish each year. When the company complained to the Chilean governor of the island, he invariably promised to punish the culprits—and invariably did nothing whatever.

Although the Chileans did supply a governor who was sent to the Isla de Pascua for a two-year stint, the post was not generally filled with the highest type of public official. (The island was considered a kind of exile.) Consequently, the governing these govenors did was usually minimal.

The Chileans also supplied a schoolteacher. The one Métraux met in 1934 was a bankrupt Chilean who had fled, using the island as a kind of hideout. Here, he doubled as teacher and public scribe. Métraux commented that the first time he met the schoolteacher, the man was unshaven and in pyjamas, and throughout the next five months "we always saw him in the same pyjamas and with the same unshaven face."

The bearded, white-robed, forty-seven-year-old Capuchin friar, Father Sebastian Englert, arrived on the island the following year, 1935. By that time, the teaching staff at the government school had doubled, for there were now two Chilean schoolteachers. The school was held for two hours in the morning for girls, and two hours in the afternoon for boys. The chief subject was the Spanish language for—from the start—the object of Chile was to Chileanize the island.

After school, according to the memory of Leonardo Pakarati, "We climbed on the statues as if they were toys. We also played with sweet potatoes. We would sculpt them into the shape of a moai; then bake them and eat them. We would pick up sea urchins on the rocks. And, of course, we all had horses."[2]

The population of small, squat mustanglike horses on Easter far outnumbered the human population which, in 1935, was a mere 450 men, women, and children. (The population growth continued in the same ratio: by 1967, there were 1,100 natives on Easter, and some 3,000 horses.) Even the poorest child could have a horse. All it required was going out and catching one, for they roamed wild on the island. Furthermore, having a horse was (and is) something of a necessity, for it is difficult to walk any distance over this island where the sharp rocks from crumbling lava blocks are strewn everywhere. (Father Sebastian put it this way: "The saying of the early rabbis that when God created the earth he had two sacks of stones in his hands, of which he dumped one over Palestine and the other over the rest of the world cannot be wholly correct. Surely God emptied at least one well-filled sack over Easter Island."[3])

Most island children learned to ride before they could walk. They straddled their horses bareback, clutching the mane or a piece of rope in front, often with a still smaller child sitting directly behind and clutching onto the first child as they galloped across a field.

For many decades, it could be said that the islanders almost lived on horseback. As late as 1962, *Life* reporter Carl Mydans wrote: "They live in a horse society, wandering about on their steeds much as the American Indians did on our prairie lands. . . . A Pascuense will sit for half a day on a horse, going nowhere, having nothing to do, much as we might sit on a rocking chair or a porch."[4]

Quite naturally, one of the first acquisitions made by Father Sebastian when he settled in on the island was a horse.

Soon after, he acquired a housekeeper-cook named Elodia Pakarati. Along with Elodia came her eleven-year-old nephew, Diego, for whom the priest developed a special affection.

On Christmas morning in 1947, Father Sebastian had celebrated the second Mass and was on his way to the leprosarium on horseback, when Diego came galloping up. The boy announced that he was going fishing in the new boat with his father, his three uncles, and his nine-year-old-brother, Mariano. It was to be a week-long expedition. They would go ashore each night, sleep in a cave, get provisions for the next day. And set out again.

Father Sebastian felt uneasy about the expedition. Diego's uncle, Domingo Pakarati, had built the largest fishing boat ever seen on the island. It was made of wood—not totora reeds—and had two sails sewn of dress fabric. There had naturally been much speculation as to why Domingo needed such a large vessel merely to go fishing off shore. (There was a strict law: No one was permitted to sail out of sight of Easter—lest an overadventurous islander should be tempted to try the suicide voyage to that eternal beacon, Tahiti.)

However, when the priest came down to see the launching —along with an enthusiastic crowd of islanders—he was convinced that the four Pakarati brothers planned to do just as they had said they would (at least on this trip). They obviously would never set out for Tahiti with two small boys aboard. Furthermore, the boat was supplied with only enough food and water for a day's outing. Every boat which had tried for Tahiti in the past had been stocked full with food supplies and tins of fresh water. Even then, the voyage almost invariably and inevitably ended in death.

For several days, the Pakarati's fishing trip went according to plan. They came ashore each night and got provisions for the next day. But one afternoon, a fierce wind swept the vessel far out to sea. The Pakaratis took down the sails, tried to row back to shore but could make no headway against the violent wind and waves. As darkness fell, the volcano tops were still visible in the distance. But by morning, there was only one terrible question: Where *was* the island? They were lost between an endless eternity of sea and sky.

The sun soon turned the small boat into a cauldron. The four men and two boys had nothing to eat but one squash. There was no fresh water at all.

"The first week out, the boys were always crying," Domingo Pakarati recounted later. "They kept remembering what they had on the island. They would say, 'Now at home they're eating watermelon.' Then they got so hungry and thirsty, they didn't cry any more. They just lay, like dead."

After eight days of attempting to find the island, Domingo decided that Tahiti might now be closer than Easter, and they should try to get there. "I figured," said Domingo, "that the sun comes from the continent and goes toward Polynesia. So we always rode with the sun at our backs in the morning, and facing into the sun in the afternoon. To judge the current and our speed, we would throw a stick from the front of the boat and count off the seconds till it reached the stern. At night, we sailed by the stars. We had to remember which stars were out *last* year at this time because in the Southern Hemisphere you see different stars at different seasons.

"Day after night after day, we sailed on. From the first day, our throats burned like fire. But there was not a drop of fresh water. If it had rained, we could have collected it in our coats. But it didn't rain once.

"When the one squash was gone, we had nothing at all to eat. We tried to fish, but we caught nothing. Sometimes flying fish would jump over the boat, whole schools of them. We prayed one would land in the boat. But it never happened.

"Somehow we survived, through thirty nights and thirty days. Then one morning, Augustin, our oldest brother, started shrieking: 'There's corn and trees and birds coming out of the trees.' I looked, and saw nothing. I was afraid he had gone mad. Then I went under the sail where he sat. And I saw it. An island.

"When we landed the people thought we were spirits. We were only skeletons covered with skin."

They had reached Reao, a small island past Tahiti. There were only 200 people on Reao. But among the 200 was a doctor. He saved the lives of the starving survivors—by not allowing them to eat or drink. They were given only a small sip of milk for the first four days. It took two months to nurse them back to health.

On September 8, 1949, the Pakaratis arrived home via a Chilean naval vessel. Their funeral services had long since been held. Now every inhabitant of the island joined in the gigantic *sau sau*—the festival feast—in their honor. It went on without stop for five nights and five days.

The Pascuenses were celebrating more than the miraculous return. The incredible story had put them in closer touch with their ancestors who also had braved the wild and perilous wastelands of the Pacific, and had somehow found their way to this loneliest island of all.

The following year the island Romeo and Juliet set forth for Tahiti. They were in love; but they were cousins—second cousins. Yet, they broke the island taboos by living together. Their families protested vehemently, and he was forced to marry another girl. In a few days, he was back—for his cousin. They could never live together on Easter Island. But if they could make it to Tahiti. . . . They took off at night, and have never been heard of since.

That same year, 1950, a Chilean pilot came to the island on a supply ship. Though no one realized it at the time, this visit of Roberto Parragué would eventually result in the ending of the perilous ocean voyages from Easter to Tahiti.

Parragué was a short, soft-spoken, friendly man who had specialized in long-range navigation. He had also organized the celestial navigation school in the Chilean Air Force. He was thirty-seven years old.

At age twenty-six, he had been the first pilot ever to round the Cape of Good Hope, in a Fairey seaplane. He was the first pilot ever to land on the so-called Robinson Crusoe island, the largest isle in the Juan Fernandez group. This dot of land (twelve miles long, two and one-half miles wide) served as the setting for the novel *Robinson Crusoe*. The island is also Easter's second closest populated neighbor; it lies 1,600 miles to the Southeast. (Easter's nearest populated neighbor is the equally tiny Pitcairn—the *Mutiny on the Bounty* island—which lies 1,300 miles to the West.)

Now, as he strode about on the stony fields, Roberto Parragué determined to become the first man ever to land a plane on Easter Island.

Other pilots considered the idea almost suicidal. It would be no easy matter to find this tiny speck of land set in a million square miles of empty ocean. One would have to fly by solar or stellar navigation, a risky business in any case. And no plane could carry·sufficient fuel to enable it to make the lengthy flight with leeway left over for hours of circling around, trying to locate the island.

Nevertheless, Parragué decided to try.

He settled on a site for the airfield: Mataveri—where the cannibal feasts had taken place after the annual Birdman Festival. Then he set off the future airstrip with stones: 1,000 feet wide and 3,000 feet long. He called some Pascuenses together; told them he would return in six months, and explained how and why they must, in the interim, clear the strip of all its stones. They promised to do so.

At noon on January 20, 1951, Parragué—now a general in the Chilean Air Force—arrived at the island and circled it in his clumsy amphibious PBY 5A. When they sighted land, his crew cheered. Parragué was the only general in the Chilean Air Force trained both as a pilot and a navigator. They knew they were in the best possible hands. Yet, few of them fully believed they would ever find the island.

As they came in for a landing, Parragué realized that the Pascuenses had done nothing whatever about clearing the airstrip which was as rocky as they day he had left. Nevertheless, he managed to set the plane down.

Rather nervously, he wondered whether the fuel he'd had sent ahead on the Chilean supply ship was still available. Perhaps the islanders had siphoned it off to use for other purposes.

He located it, however, and promptly had his plane refueled for the return trip—which he planned to make in several days.

Suddenly, two hours after the landing on Easter, it began to pour. For a month prior to Parragué's arrival, there had been a terrible drought on the island. People were forced to make the difficult trek to the volcano lake to find fresh water. But now there came the heaviest and longest rain anyone could remember. It usually rained in one section of the island at a time—a short shower. This storm however drenched the entire land, and lasted, incredibly, from two P.M. until midnight.

The next morning, Parragué discovered that a new name had been painted in large red letters on his plane: *Manutara*. Good Luck Bird. And he had been rechristened General Bird God. "The people were convinced," he said later, "that the plane and I were somehow related to the Bird God, and that we had brought the rain."

That evening a huge sau sau was held in front of the plane. As General Bird God ate his roast leg of lamb (he'd been given an entire leg), he wondered how he would ever take off from this island. The wheels of the plane were mired deep in mud.

The next day, the general ordered that the fuel be drained out of the plane, and put back into the empty oil drums (which, fortunately, had not yet been converted into a rooftop or a house siding). Then he would take off in the lightened plane, land in the ocean, and refuel there. It was a risky idea —but the only one possible.

The takeoff went according to plan. But as soon as they landed in the ocean, waves broke the right wing. As the plane tipped over, Parragué and his crew scrambled out the window and sat on the left wing. This served to create a balance but the plane promptly began to sink.

Meanwhile, help was on the way. Over one hundred Pascuenses had stripped naked and were swimming furiously to the rescue. They managed to push the crippled plane through the tremendous waves and wind to the shore.

Stout ropes were then tied to Manutara, and, singing joyously, the Pascuenses pulled the plane back to the airstrip. That night, a cow was killed under the nose of the plane, and another festive sau sau was held to celebrate the fact that Manutara had not sunk.

However, the plane's engine was waterlogged and useless,

as were all the instruments. Even General Bird God could not figure out a way to take off this time.

Fortunately, the *Pinto,* the Chilean naval vessel, was due at the island shortly for its annual supply voyage. When the *Pinto* left, the general and his crew were aboard, with their damaged plane parts.

One year later, when the next supply ship arrived at Easter, Parragué was the first passenger ashore. His luggage included a brand new engine and instruments which he had "borrowed" from the Chilean Air Force. It took him forty days to repair the plane. He was just about to take off when a Chilean warship arrived on the island—to take Parragué prisoner.

General Bird God went home in the brig.

However, when he arrived home he learned that Chile now had a new president—another general, named Ibañez.

They spoke: general to general. Parragué explained that his aim was not to steal plane parts from the Chilean Air Force, but to open Easter Island to a new era of air travel.

"You are forgiven," said General Ibañez to General Parragué, "and you can keep the plane for yourself!"

Parragué was sent to southern Chile to command an air base in Porto Montt. But he continued to push for the construction of an airstrip on Easter. Then he realized that if the Chilean government built such a strip, the chief benefactors would be Williamson, Balfour & Co. So Parragué started an all-Chilean Friends of Easter Island Club which pushed politically for the ouster of the Scottish sheep company.

In 1954, the Company's lease came up for renewal. The Chilean government refused to renew the lease. The Government did, however, offer to buy the buildings and livestock and—since there was nothing the Company could do about it—they sold.

Henceforth, the Chilean government announced, their navy

would run the sheep farm, and the profits would be used to better the lot of the islanders.

The government built a small hospital and a few dirt roads. They planted 1,000 eucalyptus trees.

The lot of the islanders, however, did not noticeably improve.

chapter 14

The following year, in October 1955, a white trawler hove into view. It circled the precipice–lined coast, and finally put in at the small stone wharf at Hanga-piko where a mysterious vehicle was brought ashore: a bright red jeep.

Father Sebastian hurried down to the shore—in time to see the ship sail away, shoved off by the heavy swell. The islanders looked disconsolate. This had happened before with many ships that had tried to land.

But the priest was certain this particular vessel would not be discouraged by the mere matter of rocky shores and violent waves. He had eagerly been awaiting the day of its arrival. This was the expedition headed by the world-famed scientist-adventurer-author, and Pacific islands expert, Thor Heyerdahl. On board were four eminent archaeologists. They had come to do what had never before been attempted on the island. They would—literally—dig deep into Easter's past. And they would attempt to date what they found. Dating had not been done by any previous expedition, for the simple reason that the carbon-14 process had not then been known.

Since the white trawler was pitching wildly on the waves, a small boat was sent out to bring Heyerdahl ashore. This last lap of the Norwegian's voyage proved to be the roughest of all. Somewhat seasick and shaky, he finally reached shore where, it seemed, all the island's 900 inhabitants had gathered.

"Ia-o-rana korua," they shouted in welcome, and the white-robed Father Sebastian came forward to greet Thor Heyerdahl.

Each man knew much about the other, and their meeting was that of immediate friends.

Then the elderly priest took Heyerdahl to meet the young Chilean governor—this time, an excellent one. The three men decided that the scientists should set up their tent camp at Anakena, where Hotu Matua had first landed. This would mean traveling to the sheep farm headquarters at Vaitea in the middle of the island for all firewood and drinking water (which the British had piped in from the volcano lake in Rano Aroi). However, the isolated beach was the most beautiful site on the island. Furthermore, the farther the expedition tents were from the village of Hanga-roa, the less likelihood there would be of "the spirits" appropriating things.

Heyerdahl and a few others visited the beach and pronounced it ideal. They would be living in the very shadow of the ancient islanders. There were three high-terraced ahus, with gigantic moai lying before them, faces in the dirt. The highest ahu had but a single statue which had been shoved off its altar, a broad-shouldered giant who looked imposing, even lying prone. This massive stone man was stretched out by the foundations of King Hotu Matua's beachfront house.

The green tents of the new temporary residents were set out on the flat plaza where prehistoric islanders had once danced and feasted and lit fires as they worshipped before the towering ancestral images.

Although the archaeologists had come to dig, one question loomed large: Was there sufficient soil on Easter to make meaningful "digs" possible? The other South Sea islands had once been heavily wooded. But if this island had always been as treeless as the early discoverers described it, if there had been no rotting vegetation to make stratas of soil pile up year by year, then there would be little to dig into. The fact that the foundations of Hotu Matua's house still showed above-ground was not an encouraging sign.

It was Mrs. Heyerdahl who gave the first clue that digging on the island might prove to be rewarding after all. Like many a housewife at home, she ran her forefinger over the bookshelf and made a clean streak through the dust which had gathered there in a few days' time. Her husband was delighted. As he put it; "In a hundred years or so, there would be a pretty thick layer to brush away."

The selection of the first excavation site was an obvious one: the cave dwelling and the boat-shaped house of the island's legendary first king.

As the archaeologists carefully shook earth through their fine-meshed nets, they came across fishhooks of human bone, human teeth, and charcoal; they were speculating on just how far back through the centuries they had dug when Dr. William Mulloy (Professor and Head of the Department of Archaeology at the University of Wyoming) discovered a small bluish-green glass bead.

The island's discoverer, Roggoveen, had written in his log-book that they had given two strings of blue beads to the first native who boarded their ship. Was this a remnant of that gift made in 1772? In any case, the archaeologists knew that they had not dug deeper than the eighteenth century.

Hotu Matua's homestead yielded no further signs of human activity. But it had proved one thing: There were sufficient soil layers to make digging on Easter very worthwhile.

The next dig proved to be an archaeologist's dream come true.

Visitors from Captain Cook onward were awed and amazed at the precise stonework in the ancient ahus. In 1774, Cook wrote: "The workmanship is not inferior to the best plain piece of masonry we have in England. They use no cement, yet the joints are exceedingly close, and the stones morticed and tenanted one into another, in a very artful manner."

Dr. Mulloy had selected as his exploration site the ceremonial center at Vinapu which lay in a valley on the southeastern shore of the island. The small, steep, beachlike frontage was carpeted with smooth, sea-worn pebbles which were washed back and forth by the waves, providing a steady rhythm of timelessness which Mulloy called "awe-inspiring."

Awe-inspiring also were the three huge ahus at the ceremonial site, the finest altars on the island. They were faced with blocks of smooth-finished, perfectly fitted stones; some were small, and some weighed more than five tons each. They were set together, without mortar, in a masonry technique so remarkable that, in most places, it was impossible to fit a penknife blade between the stones. As Mulloy put it when describing Ahu No. 1:

> The meticulous attention to foundation, footing and the precise fitting of each individual stone has produced a structure all but impervious to the forces of nature. . . .
> It seems probable that the structure was completely conceived and planned before it was begun, with a real feeling for balance and symmetry. . . . Those who did it were artists as well as craftsmen.[1]

Mulloy also discovered that the ahu planners were astronomers, for the placement of the three Vinapu ahus was related to the position of the rising sun at the equinoxes and the summer and winter solstices.

Furthermore, the ceremonial center was the site of two villages of boat-shaped houses—villages which once had been guarded and shadowed by the huge stone giants which stood on the ahus—some fifteen of them, replete with topknots. All now lay face in the dirt amid rubble and plaza stones.

The archaeologists fully expected that excavations in the Vinapu Ceremonial Site would yield interesting results. But they did not expect that the revelations would turn Easter Island history upside down and inside out.

It had always been assumed that the fine masonry of the ahus was created by the men who made the moais. It had also been generally assumed that the ahus were made by Polynesians who came originally from the Asian mainland. Since Easter lay farther from Asia than any other Pacific island, and since Polynesia was known to be the last area of the globe to be settled, it was estimated that the first inhabitants arrived on Easter in the fourteenth century A.D.—at the earliest. Some put the date at 1500 or 1600 A.D.

But the archaeologists proved otherwise. Mulloy's excavations at the Vinapu ahus, backed up by carbon-14 datings—and further borne out by other ahu excavations done at the same time by the other archaeologists—proved that the ahus had been built by men who settled on the island long before the era of the Statuemakers.

The earliest radiocarbon date of unquestioned reliability came from Dr. Mulloy's excavations at Ahu No. 2 at Vinapu. It showed that men had built fires there in 857 A.D. (plus or minus 200 years). Since the first settlers presumably spent some time settling on the island before starting work on the ahus, it can be said with some certainty that, as Dr. Mulloy put it: "Sometime before 800 A.D., these people began to develop by far the most remarkable religious building compulsion known in the whole Pacific."

(A far earlier carbon dating was turned up at Poike Ditch: 380 A.D., plus or minus 100 years. But this is not regarded by archaeologists as a dating of "unquestioned reliability.")

Dr. Mulloy also discovered that there were three distinct periods of Easter's Stone Age history.

The ahu builders came first. Where did they come from? Heyerdahl was convinced that the Vinapu altars themselves gave the answer. There was a striking similarity between these structures and those built by the Inca Indians—or their predecessors. No such altars had been found on any of the tens of thousands of other islands in the Pacific. And Easter was the island which lay closest to the land of the Incas. If the first settlers came from the west coast of South America, Easter would have been the first Polynesian island settled, instead of the last. And the ahu builders would have imported their construction skills from "the Old World."

The early altars scattered along the seacoast were varied. But the most typical had a long, narrow platform with a sloping stone ramp on one side. Facing the ramp was a plaza, a leveled area, sometimes enclosed with earthen embankments. And beyond it, boat-shaped houses, presumably used by priests.

Some of the ahus on the island were over 150 yards long. Their height and size undoubtedly reflected the numbers and status of the kin group that built them.

The archaeologists could find no "closing date" for the Early Period. But Mulloy's excavations at Vinapu clearly showed that, at the end of the Early Period, the ahus were no longer "kept up"; indeed, many of the stones were removed, probably for use elsewhere.

The Middle Period was that of the statuemakers, who rebuilt the ahus to serve as fitting altars for their giant stone men. The masonry differed distinctly from that of the Early Period. It was often crude, and lacked symmetry. If an altar was strong enough to hold the moai, that was sufficient. Some ahus held a single statue. Others held as many as sixteen.

Although Mulloy found no specific starting-date clue for the Middle Period, his co-worker, Dr. Arne Skjölsvold, did. He was a Norwegian archaeologist, head of the new state museum at Elverum. The earliest carbon-14 dating he discovered at the Rano Raraku quarry was 1206 A.D. By taking a midway point between the Vinapu's earliest Early Period date—857 A.D.—and the earliest statue-making date, the Heyerdahl expedition archaeologists arrived at "an arbitrary commencement date" for the Middle Period: 1100 A.D. The ending date of the Middle Period was far more specific: 1680, the year of the Poike Ditch fire.

Then came the Late Period—the statue-overthrowing-Time: the era of the warriors and the cannibals, which lasted from 1680 until the arrival of the missionaries in 1868. Not only were statues thrown down, but attempts were made to destroy the altars as well.

Along with the destruction came a new use for the ahu. Although the dead had previously been cremated in special structures at the ahu, the altars themselves now served as burial sites. Corpses were set out on the platforms—or in the shadow of a fallen statue—and covered with a pile of stones. Or, uncovered bodies were left to rot away. When only a skeleton remained, the bones were stuck into holes and crevices made by other stones piled on the altar. Many ancient ahus took on the appearance of a pile of stones. Then new ahus were built as burial places; they, too, were only a long and narrow heap of stones.

Dr. William Mulloy, aided by some twenty islanders, worked at the Vinapu Ceremonial Site from November 27, 1955 to April 6, 1956. During these weeks, he unearthed a timetable of the island's ancient history, and he proved that the first settlers to leave a lasting mark had built their remarkable ahus centuries before the statuemakers started to fashion their massive ancestral images.

Meanwhile, Dr. Arne Skjölsvold and his team of islanders were hard at work on the cliffs of Rano Raraku. One day while traversing the southwest corner of the territory, the scientist stopped short and did a double take. Were those *eyes* looking up at him from the volcanic tuff? Natives had been climbing these rocks for centuries. Yet no one had noticed these strange, oval-shaped eyes.

Excavation was started at once. It was not difficult. The statue had been buried by rubble from the quarry. When this was removed, the full-bodied figure of a kneeling man stared up. And the natives and scientists stared back. This statue was completely different from any ever found on Easter Island. The head looked nothing like the elongated, long-eared, beardless moai. This kneeling man had a short, neat goatee; short ears; and a naturalistic, rounded-shaped head.

As for the body, instead of being cut off at the torso with fingers touching at the belly, this kneeling figure was all there —with plump backside resting on its heels, and hands neatly on its knees. Furthermore, all the moai on Rano Raraku were blind—except for this statue where the eyes were carefully hollowed out; each pupil was marked by pecked-out holes.

The statue was moved from a prone to an upright position —with the aid of the red jeep, chains, ropes, tackle, poles, and the manpower of twenty natives. (This merely to raise a ten-ton stone man. He was a midget compared to most of the moai.)

When he knelt on the volcano slope, virtually every inhabitant of Easter came to gaze at him in wonder. Nothing like him had ever been seen by any of them. But something very like him *had* been seen by Heyerdahl, by Skjölsvold, and by Gonzalo Figueroa (the handsome young archaeology student from Santiago University who had come on the mission as the official representative of Chile). There was a remarkable resemblance between this kneeling statue and some they had seen in the old Andean culture area of Tiahuanaco: the same posture, the same head, the same large, oval eyes, the same lips and rounded cheeks, and the same small goatee.

Tiahuanaco lay at the top of the world, close to the shores of Lake Titicaca. It was the oldest pre-Inca culture center known. Indeed, when the Incas arrived there, they found altars made like the Vinapu ahus—statues like the kneeling men. But the altar builders and the statuemakers had departed before the Incas came and the legends said that they were the long-eared, red-haired, bearded white men who had disappeared in huge canoes over the Pacific horizon.

The archaeologists unearthed several other statues, less well preserved, but obviously related to the kneeling man and not the moai. They assumed that all of these pre-Inca-style statues had been made during the Early Period by the ahu builders.

But who were the men who had made the "traditional" Easter Island moai?

Were they a new group of immigrants, Polynesians perhaps, who had come to the island with Hotu Matua?

Or perhaps, after living on the island for centuries, cut off from the rest of the world by the horizon line, the original South American settlers had eventually forgotten their Tiahuanaco culture and had developed their own absolutely unique Easter Island moai.

It was certain, however, that at some point, bona fide Polynesians had settled on the island: a brown-skinned, black-haired, flat-nosed people. They comprised the chief racial stock when Roggoveen discovered Easter in 1772. Were they the Short Ears?

But the kneeling statue and his stone relatives also had short ears. If they had been fashioned by the long-eared, red-haired white men from South America, why did they not have long ears? Or perhaps, only some of the original settlers lengthened their lobes; the statuemakers did not.

Or had there been three groups of settlers:
- the pre-Incas from the west coast of South America;
- followed by long-eared Polynesians, perhaps from the Marquesas (where ear-lobe-stretching was also in vogue);
- and then the final group of settlers—the short-eared Polynesians, who served first as workers and then murderers of the Long Ears and of the remarkable civilization which flourished on the island?

The unearthing of a three-epoch timetable did not, in the minds of most Easter Island experts, bring any conclusive answers to the perplexing question as to where the islanders came from, and when each contingent had arrived.

Heyerdahl, however, was certain that he and his archaeologists had found proof positive of the origins of the most ancient settlers of Easter Island. And before he left the island, he discovered still more eloquent proof which did, indeed, seem to be irrefutable.

But first, Thor Heyerdahl was hit with an inspiration which led to the dramatic unveiling of other puzzling mysteries.

chapter 15

Heyerdahl had met the native mayor of Easter Island. Indeed, it would have been impossible not to meet this enterprising gentleman, who had been among the first aboard the trawler when it neared shore. The mayor came, not in his official capacity, but to sell his wooden statues. He was, he explained, the finest wood-carver on the island. His name was Pedro Atan.

This same Atan had also been among the first to board Métraux's ship in 1934—for the same purpose. And when Métraux told Pedro of his interest in ancient objects, the young man blandly informed him: "There aren't many ancient objects about nowadays and it will take time to find them. But don't worry, we'll make you as many as you want. We'll give you whatever you ask for. When you get home, nobody will know the difference."[1]

Both Métraux and Heyerdahl at first regarded the thin, smiling Pedro with his small mustache as somewhat of a lightweight—a clown. But it turned out that this same Pedro Atan—at Heyerdahl's request—organized the revelation of answers to three island mysteries: how the moai were made; how they were raised; and how they were transported unscathed across the countryside.

The Norwegian's first inspiration came when he spent a night with the moai on Rano Raraku. He found what looked like an ideal bunk: a long empty space from which a statue had been removed. This "canopy bed" was, however, uncomfortably hard. This led Heyerdahl to wonder anew *how* the huge stone men had been carved by natives with no use of metal tools. The skipper of the trawler had come to the quarry and after working hard for a half an hour with a large hammer and chisel, had managed only to loosen a piece of rock the size of his fist. How long then would it have taken the ancient statuemakers with their small rock picks to chip off the same fist-size piece? How long would it have taken them to make a moai?

Heyerdahl decided he would try to find out.

The next morning, he consulted Father Sebastian about his idea: starting work in the old quarry again. The twentieth-century statuemakers should be, if possible, the descendants of the last Long Ear, Ororoina. The priest was enthusiastic and informed Heyerdahl that there was only one family on the island descended in a direct line from Ororoina—the Atan family which had selected the imposing surname Adam when Christianity was introduced on the island. The natives pronounced it Atam, or Atan. The senior member of the family was the mayor, Pedro—a direct descendant from Ororoina on his father's side.

The mayor took to the idea of working the quarry at once. He and five other Long Ears would build a medium-sized moai, fifteen to twenty feet high.

The night before the moai-making was to start, a strange ceremony took place. The Long Ears gathered in the darkness and sang an eerie song as they bowed and swayed and beat time with wooden paddles. The men wore crowns of leaves, and there were two small children present, each wearing a paper mask representing a birdman with large eyes and long beak.

The Mayor later told the archaeologists that this was the old stonecutters' song, asking their most important god, Atua, for good luck in the work they were about to begin.

The next morning the Twentieth-Century Long Ears set to work. They had gathered up a heap of obsidian picks, had sharpened them well, and each man was supplied with dozens. Each sculptor also had a gourdful of water beside him. Then the Mayor marked out measurements for the new moai, and, upon signal, the sculptors burst into their stonecutters' song and started striking the rock with their small picks in the song's rhythm. Water was splashed onto the stone to lessen the chance of splinters flying into their eyes.

The mayor acted as coordinator, and obsidian-pick-sharpener. He worked quickly, so the five sculptors always had sharp tools on hand. In a steady assembly line of motion, the men hammered at the rock, flung water, changed picks, and by the third day, the shape of the new moai could clearly be seen.

By the end of that day, the Long Ears complained that they were wood-carvers not stone-carvers. The callouses on their fingers hurt and they wanted to stop. Calculations were made, and it was decided that it would take six men one year to make a fifteen-ton moai.

A halt was called to the statue making. But Heyerdahl had another project to present to the mayor. He offered Atan one hundred dollars on the day the broad-shouldered statue at Anakena stood on its ahu. The only equipment permissible was that which would have been available to the ancient moai movers.

The mayor accepted eagerly. This time, he rounded up twelve Long Ears. Their nighttime singing and dancing was eerie, elaborate, and entirely different from the stonecutters' song and ceremony. The next day, they came with three wooden poles (permissible, since—according to the early explorers—trees had always grown around the crater lake in Rano Kao). The natives had also gathered a large pile of stones.

Once again, the mayor played the leading role. As the other Long Ears pushed the ends of their poles under the statue's buried face and then leaned on the poles to lever the head up a fraction, Pedro Atan stretched out in the sand and shoved small stones under the moai's face.

By evening, the statue's head had been raised one yard, and it lay on a pillow of stones.

The next day, the mayor appointed one of his brothers as official stone shover, and he stood on the ahu wall directing the operation. First, the right side would be levered up a little, and stones placed underneath. Then the process was repeated on the left side.

After nine days, the statue lay prone on a tower of stones so high that the polemen had to hang from ropes fastened to the end of the levers.

The rest of the operation was watched with increasing nervousness by the archaeologists, and by Mrs. Heyerdahl who now stopped two-year-old Anette from bringing stones to the mayor in her baby carriage. A single carelessly placed boulder could bring the twenty-five-ton statue rolling down.

Sweating, near-naked men came staggering along, carrying huge boulders. Others scrambled up the rock pile to shove each massive stone in place. The mayor, seemingly unaware of the risks, called out orders with assurance and aplomb. And, despite the fact that shotlike sounds rang out at intervals as rocks cracked under the statue's weight, the moai kept rising slowly, steadily until—on the eighteenth day—it was ready, said the mayor, to be moved onto its ahu.

The Island mayor used the remarkable methods of his ancestors to raise this moai. It was the first statue to be raised in modern times.

Atan directed that ropes be attached to the statue's forehead and neck. These were firmly anchored to prevent the stone giant from toppling over at this final crucial phase in the operations. Then, as men pulled on the ropes and pressed on the two pole levers under its chin, the moai almost magically began to move upright.

And, suddenly, there it was—in place on its ahu, looming

over the landscape—the first maoi to stand upright on Easter Island since the Statue-overthrowing-Time.

How had the mayor been so certain of the method by which the statues were raised? When Heyerdahl asked him, Pedro Atan replied that his grandfather and his grandfather's brother-in-law, old Porotu, had taught him this and other secrets of the ancients when he was a small boy.

And why had Atan never told anyone how the statues were raised?

"No one," said the mayor, "ever asked me."

The matter of the topknot-raising suddenly lost its mystery when looking at the mountain of stones beside the standing moai. Though the prehistoric islanders did not use the wheel, the topknots were, after all, cylindrical, and could have been rolled from the quarry to the statue to be adorned. Then, with ropes, they could, presumably, be maneuvered into place using—as a ramp—the same pile of stones which had been collected to raise the moai. When the job was done, and all the stones carted away, the mystery would clearly spring into being: How *had* the red topknot been set on the giant's head?

Heyerdahl next asked the mayor whether he knew how the moai had been moved for miles over the stony landscape. And the mayor answered in the traditional manner: Imbued with mana, the statues stood up and walked to their chosen ahu. When pressed, however, Atan came up with a more practical idea. His grandfather and old Porotu had told him that heavy ahu boulders had been moved by means of a thick Y-shaped

Children of Easter Island play in and on the red stone cylinders which their ancestors carved as "topknots" for the towering statues.

tree branch with a crosspiece, forming a sort of sledge. Perhaps such a device, plus heavy ropes made from *hau hau* bark, plus a good deal of manpower, *could* move a moai. He agreed to try. But this time the operation could not be limited to Long Ears. They must muster all the pulling power they could.

Since payment in the ancient days had consisted of food and feasts, Heyerdahl decided to try the same lure. Two oxen were slaughtered and roasted in a huge earth oven—near a ten-ton moai which had just been discovered and dug up by the archaeologists. All the men, women, and children in Hanga-roa were invited to gorge themselves on hunks of steaming steak, corn on the cob, and the inevitable sweet potatoes. After the feast—complete with guitars and hula dancing—180 islanders started hauling jubilantly on the rope which had been fastened around the neck of the newly unearthed moai. The rope promptly broke, which added to the hilarity of the occasion.

Undaunted, the mayor ordered the rope doubled. And this time, as the horde of enthusiastic girls and men pulled with all their might—the moai moved, at first, jerkily. Then, on its forked tree-trunk sledge, it started sliding with surprising speed over the stony field. Suddenly, the mystery of moving the moai across the island seemed to vanish into the sunny blue afternoon. If 180 well-fed men and women could pull a ten-ton statue across a field, quite obviously an increasing number of haulers could transport the massive fifty or eighty-ton moai.

There may, of course, have been other means of statue moving.

Dr. Mulloy put forth the theory that some of the more pot-bellied models may have been moved along by ropes in a semiupright position with their plump stomachs acting as a fulcrum for the slightly rolling motion of the stone man.

And then a further moving means was discovered.

Among Easter's mysteries were the paved roads leading down to the sea. These roads, in fact, formed the chief "evidence" for those Easter Island aficionados who insisted that the island was the sole remaining mountaintop tip of a lost continent where a great civilization had once flourished. The paved roads, they were certain, were "continued" many fathoms deep on the ocean floor. (They conveniently ignored the fact that oceanographers, after taking deposits from the Pacific bottom, proved that there had been no notable upheavals or sinkings of land masses in the Polynesian part of the Pacific since the emergence of man on our planet.)

But why had the anicent paved roads been built running straight down to the ocean's edge? The old name for these roads were *apapa*, meaning "unload." Paymaster William Thomson had noted these "peculiar ways, made by paving the sloping bank with regular lines of smooth, round boulders, as though intended for hauling up heavy boats or weights." However, he concluded, "As far as known, the images were never transported by sea, nor did the islanders possess boats sufficiently large to float them or material from which they could be constructed."[2]

This assumption was generally accepted—until the arrival of Heyerdahl and his archaeologists. They discovered one apapa on the south coast at the foot of a large ahu. The paved road led to an inlet chock-full of boulders. But among these black rocks lay three huge red topknots. What were the topknots doing in the water? They must have been brought there by boat. Apapa. Unload. But obviously, the boat had sunk before these ten-ton "wigs" could be unloaded.

However, what kind of boat could the ancients have built that would have held a ten-ton topknot?

Edwin Ferdon of the Anthropology Division of the Museum of New Mexico found an answer.

Dr. Ferdon had picked the cliff-edge ceremonial center of Orongo for his exploration site. He was fascinated by the ancient evidences of sun worship and knowledge of astronomy which he found there: neatly bored holes in the rocks which lined up perfectly with the sunrise at the summer and winter solstices; an ahu with a sundial marking the position of the rising sun at the equinoxes; an accurate solar calendar. Hyerdahl emphatically pointed out that the ancient Incas and their predecessors had also been sun-worshippers and oriented many of their religious structures according to the solstices.

Then Ferdon found something which brought the Norwegian back to Orongo on the run.

Heyerdahl had been investigating island caves where tribes had hidden out during the Statue-overthrowing-Time, and secret "Family Caves" where he had been told magic stone sculptures were hidden. Some of these caves were decorated with wall paintings.

At Orongo, there were caves of a different sort with wall paintings of birdmen and decorated ceremonial paddles. These ceremonial caves were marked by an entranceway of flat stone slabs.

At the seeming risk of being crushed to death, Ferdon explored the Orongo caves. In one of them, he found an ancient wall painting of a crescent-shaped boat with square sails. It was then that he sent for Heyerdahl—who gazed at the painting with high excitement.

He had seen boats exactly like this at Lake Titicaca—the highest navigable lake in the world. Lake Titicaca—near the pre-Inca culture center of Tiahuanaco in the Andes Mountains borderland between Bolivia and Peru. And he had been told that the crescent-shaped, square-sailed boats were used by the red-haired, white-skinned, long-eared men who had been there before the Incas arrived. The boats were made of woven totora reeds.

Totora. This rare and distinctive freshwater reed was unknown on the islands of the Pacific—with one exception. It grew in profusion in and around the three freshwater crater lakes in the volcanoes of Easter Island. Roggoveen and other early chroniclers had noted that totora was widely used by the natives for everything from shrouds for the dead to siding for the boat-shaped houses.

And, from his visit to the pre-Inca centers at Tiahuanaco, Heyerdahl knew that totora could also be used to make crescent-shaped boats which were able to carry massive blocks of rock weighing up to one hundred tons each. He had seen such carved blocks in the remains of the ancient pre-Inca roadway leading from Lake Titicaca to Tiahuanaco. And he had visited the extinct volcano of Kapia across Lake Titicaca where the blocks had been hewn. There was only one way to transport them across the thirty-mile lake. By boat—the gigantic crescent-shaped boats made of woven totora reeds.

Totora-reed boats—which could also have carried topknots and even moai around the Easter Island shoreline, to be unloaded at apapa at the foot of the coastal ahu. Totora reed boats—which could have carried colonizers from the shores of pre-Inca Peru across the Pacific to Easter Island.

As Dr. Ferdon's flashlight brought the red-and-white-painted crescent-shaped boat into brightness on the wall of an Orongo cliff-top cave, Heyerdahl said quietly: "Ed, do you know the name of the mountain by the old pre-Inca road which leads from Lake Titicaca to Tiahuanaco? They call it the Navel of the World."

chapter 16

Heyerdahl and Company left Easter Island on April 6, 1956, having spent six months casting a revealing light on the long-buried dark ages of the island's prehistoric people. As they sailed away, Anette Heyerdahl, age two and one-half ran excitedly around the deck (in the words of archaeologist Smith) "saying foul things in Spanish, English, and Pascuense."

The expedition left behind its red jeep, money to build a new church, and the fervent good will of the islanders who begged them to return.

Four years later, two of them did. The anthropologists, Mulloy and Figueroa, spent eight months first excavating, and then restoring, the ahu and moai at Akivi, three miles from Hanga-roa. This ahu was unusual in that it was inland. Most of the other altars which held statues rimmed the coastline.

Restoration of the Akivi ahu transformed it from a crude-looking platform of stones and sun-bleached human bones to a splendid edifice, eighty yards long, astronomically oriented, and a structure with beautifully fitted Vinapu-like masonry. Furthermore, the ahu revealed the same three epochs as had been found at Vinapu.

Then using the method of moai-raising shown them by the

The seven stone giants of Akivi were set back on their ahu by archaeologists Molloy and Figueroa in 1960.

mayor, the archaeologists raised the sixteen-ton, fourteen-foot-
high statues and set them back on their ahu. Once again, they
stood upright, impassive, eternal; towering over the landscape; dwarfing even the sloping swells of the cinder-cone hills
far behind them. Seven stone giants stark against an endless
sky.

There were now eight stone statues standing on the island
—staring, it seemed, back into the past. But the islanders

themselves started looking ahead to the future. And the outside world slowly began moving in.

General Bird God came back with a special commission of engineers to select the best place for a new airstrip. The Chilean national airline, Lan-Chile, had bought four DC6Bs, planning to open a new South Pacific route, island-hopping from Easter to Tahiti. After tramping all over the island, the commission members came to the conclusion that the best place for the airstrip would be the site Roberto Parragué had selected on his 1950 visit They went back home to make their report.

In 1961, the Pascuenses took sides in the Cold War—basing their political policies on cigarettes. Their economy *had* been based, as Dr. Mulloy put it, "on politeness. Particularly so far as food went. If you needed some food, you asked your neighbor." Actual money meant very little. *National Geographic* reporter Howard La Fay who visited the island in 1961 recounted that one Sunday morning he stood before the church waiting for Mass to begin and spotted a Chilean banknote lying on the plaza. Since ninety-seven percent of the islanders come to church on Sunday, the plaza was well populated. People looked at the money, but no one bothered to pick it up. La Fay asked, "Why doesn't anyone pick up that bill?" He was told: "What for? It will buy nothing here."[1]

The Chilean supply ship still showed up only once a year, and the sole store on the island was still the government-sponsored ECA. The islanders were, consequently, at the mercy of the memory or the whims of the Chilean supply agent. For one entire year, for example, they went without matches; the agent had forgotten to send them. And even when his memory served him well, the store soon ran out of supplies—which was why money was of little moment.

Cigarettes, however, were another matter. Everyone wanted

them. They had become, therefore, the island's unofficial currency. They were obtained chiefly by bartering wood carvings with sailors on those ships which very occasionally anchored offshore. When a Russian oceanographic vessel visited Easter, the wood-carvers returned from their visit aboard elated with their many cartons of Russian cigarettes. But it turned out that the cartons contained *papirosy,* with three-inch mouthpieces and a mere inch of tobacco. The enraged islanders promptly became anti-Russian.

Several years later, the islanders took a further step toward modernity. They had a revolution.

Customarily, the Chilean governor selected seven Pascuense elders to serve as the Legislature. He appointed one of the seven elders as mayor. But the islanders suddenly decided they had had enough of elders. They wanted a younger. Indeed, they wanted one particular younger, a handsome twenty-two-year-old Pascuense schoolteacher who had been educated in Chile and now returned to the island bursting with new ideas—among them the conception that the Pascuense mayor should have as much say in the running of the island as the governor. This delighted the Pascuenses, and in a completely unauthorized election, the young schoolteacher, Alfonso Rapu, was elected mayor.

The governor, of course, did not go along. He accused Rapu (quite mistakenly, as it turned out) of instigating the Bulldozer Sabotage. (The Valparaiso Public Works Department had loaned the island a bulldozer, which was scheduled to be returned on the Chilean supply ship then in port. To forestall this, islanders stole some crucial parts so the bulldozer could not be moved.)

The governor had at his disposal a contingent of mounted Chilean policeman, thirty of them, who rode about every day in full uniform—with nothing to do. For two years preceding their Rapu assignment, the only person to be jailed on the island was a drunken Chilean workman. His crime: brandishing a penknife. But now the policemen were ordered to track down Rapu—who had fled to the hills— and arrest him so that he could be deported to Chile.

Before fleeing, Rapu managed to smuggle a letter aboard the supply ship. It was addressed to the President of Chile— with copies to Chilean newspapers. It described the plight of the Pascuenses and hinted that the islanders might opt to join a Polynesian federation headed by Tahiti. The newspapers blew up the letter with ever-ballooning rumors, including one in which the Chilean governor and all his family had, supposedly, been murdered by the rampaging Pascuenses. Such an uproar ensued in Chile that the president sent forty marines to the island aboard a warship. When the rifle squads landed —backed by jeeps and heavy weapons units—they were met by a horde of singing Pascuenses. The women hugged and kissed the strangers (as was their wont when greeting visitors) and hung flowered leis over their helmets.

Having thus secured the island, the marine commander sent his men out in jeeps to search for the runaway "revolutionary" Rapu. But the islanders were not worried. "Only Pascuenses know the caves," they said. "We've been hiding out in them since the days of Hotu Matua."

Finally, however, Rapu got tired of hiding out, and he reported in to the marine commander. More rumors exploded: Alfonso would be deported to Chile. Whereupon, the mayor was recaptured by hundreds of screaming women, who vowed the Chileans would never get him. The governor gave in. Official elections were held. Women were allowed to vote, which, of course, ensured that the handsome Rapu would win by a landslide. He became mayor—for the *escudo* equivalent of $1.40 a month. And he immediately began pressing for more Pascuense rights.

More pressure came, unexpectedly, from another source. A French writer-adventurer-filmmaker named Francis Mazière landed in his yacht and asked the governor for permission to make archaeological excavations on the island. The governor refused on the grounds that the Frenchman was not an archaeologist. Mazière was miffed. He published a book, *Le Mistaire de l'Isle de Pasque*—which described Easter as "the world's last concentration camp." This caused quite a stir in Europe. The author then went about lecturing on the plight of the islanders. He spoke so dramatically that ladies in the audience often left weeping. He was guilty of gross exaggeration. But it was undeniably true that Chile had been guilty of gross neglect.

In response to the various pressures—including some from the all-Chilean Friends of Easter Island—the Chilean government passed an Easter Island Act on Feburary 1965. The islanders were given their long-awaited due which included voting rights both on the island and in Chile, social security and socialized medicine. Not everything was free, however. The new Chilean dentist charged the equivalent of twenty-five dollars for a set of uppers. And the doctor was so inexperienced that even the governor called the midwife when he was sick.

Eight Chilean nuns were sent to teach in the school. (Two volunteered for the leprosarium.) With Rapu and his beautiful new bride, Carmen, this brought the teaching staff at the school to a respectable number for the ever-increasing island population of children. (It was said that children were Easter's main crop. Some women had as many as fourteen to sixteen offspring.)

When the Easter Island Act was passed, Chile redoubled her drive to "Chileanize" the Pascuense population which numbered about 1,000. In order to encourage more Chileans to move to the island, *Continentales* were offered a 200 per

cent increase in salary for working on the island. The Pascuenses heard about this, demanded—and got—a 200 per
cent increase, too. Though the money meant little to the
islanders, it did appeal to the Chileans, and, within months, it
attracted some 400 of them to the island.

On March 1, 1966, the administration of Isla de Pascua
was removed from the responsibilities of the Chilean navy. By
Decree #16441, it became a department of Valparaiso (along
with Sala y Gomez, a tiny speck of a Southeastern Pacific
island, inhabited only by sea birds). A Chilean civilian administration took over on Easter. The *New York Times* reported
that it was no more popular with the Pascuenses than the naval
administration had been. Nevertheless, thanks in large measure to the prodding and planning of Mayor Rapu, the life and
the lot of the islanders did improve. Rapu organized a fishing
and a farming cooperative. The Chileans cooperated by setting
up an agricultural station: 10,000 square yards planted with
flowers from Samoa, sugar cane, beans, guava, and seven
styles of bananas. The Chilean agronomist reported that the
soil was good; there were only three problems: too many
stones, crickets, and *cucaleca*—a very hungry type of worm.

The new Chilean governor was an engineer. He had three
wells dug, and water was piped into town. The people were
no longer dependent on roof-top cisterns for catching rain-
water.

Zoning laws were put into effect in Hanga-roa. Every house
had to have thirty square feet of garden, and all newlyweds
were given a free house and a small plot of land on the out-
skirts of town. There were no taxes of any sort for anyone.

Then in October 1966, the U.S. Air Force arrived—in the
person of fifty-eight men who came to set up a research station
on Rano Kau for the purpose of studying the ionosphere.
They immediately hired forty Pascuenses and taught them

Zoning laws insist on greenery and garden for each house in Hanga-roa.

carpentry, mechanics, driving, English—and the Twist. The Americans and their Pascuense helpers built a prefabricated base in twenty-three days. They also installed a generator for their own use. But it meant that many Pascuenses now had several hours of electricity a day—for the first time. Suddenly the islanders discovered something they could buy with their accumulated savings. The next supply ship that came from the mainland was loaded with prepaid washing machines and refrigerators.

The U.S. Air Force then suggested to the Chilean government that an airstrip was needed on Easter. Indeed, they did more than suggest: They gave the money to build the strip. The Chileans had been sending a new commission every year to study the matter and make a report. But now, within two months, the airstrip was built.

On April 7, 1967, the first airborne flight of tourists arrived on the island—in a DC-6B piloted by General Bird God Roberto Parragué, who by now was a director of the country's national airline, Lan-Chile.

The tourists had come to Easter via a strange and circuitous route. An adventurous and irrepressible tour operator named Lars-Eric Lindblad specialized in places which made ordinary "off-the-beaten-track" itineraries sound like a trip down Main Street. While Lindblad was in Chile negotiating for a ship to go to Antarctica, he heard about the new airstrip on Easter Island and asked if he could arrange for a tourist expedition. He was given an unequivocal, "Impossible." But Lindblad was not one to take impossible for an answer. After his return from Antarctica, he boarded the first civilian plane ever to land on Easter Island (piloted, of course, by Parragué). Having finally won the approval of the Chilean government for his venture, he made arrangements for tents, tour trucks, and other supplies to be brought on the next Chilean supply ship, and for flush toilets and hot and cold showers to be built on a site overlooking the ocean. He was a bit taken aback when the governor informed him that he must have a casino. "Well," said Lindblad, "we're not quite ready for *that* yet." But *casino,* in Spanish means restaurant. And that was built, too. He also arranged for three of the "Heyerdahl archaeologists," Drs. Mulloy, Smith, and Figueroa, to serve as tour guides on the first and the second tourist expeditions to Easter Island.

The news that tourists had landed on Easter brought shudders to the souls of the many thousands throughout the world who liked to muse on the island's mysteries, safe in the belief that the geographical isolation of the island made this one Polynesian haven protected from the incursions of modern civilization.

But, during the four weeks between the arrival of the first tourist expedition (April 8, 1967) and the departure of the second tourist expedition (May 8), tourism may be said to have saved some of the most unique aspects of the island. During the first tourist expedition, Lindblad and Dr. Mulloy discovered to their horror that the governor was proudly building "a scenic coastal road" around the island. Not only was the road cutting unconcernedly close to ancient ahu plazas, but the conveniently large and exposed stones of the plazas and boat-shaped houses were being ground up to make a rock layer for the road bed.

They also discovered that the Chilean head of the agricultural experimental station had started to "surprise the governor" by raising two of the twenty-ton moai. He planned to place them neatly as a "set" on each side of the road at the entrance to his domain. And the Valparaiso bulldozer was creating a parking lot—for the island's dozen motor vehicles —in the center of one of the most archaeologically interesting and beautiful coastal sites.

Fortunately, however, none of this desecration had gone too

The first tent camp for tourists set up in 1967.

far. When Mulloy and Lindblad returned to Santiago with the first tourist expedition, they reported at once to top officials of the government. There was an immediate top-level scandal. All roadwork and such was ordered stopped until the second tourist expedition arrived with the Chilean archaeologist, Gonzalo Figueroa, who was appointed by the government to make a careful study in order to determine where the roads could go without interfering with archaeological sites.

A further result of the Lindblad-Mulloy report was the

setting up in Chile of a *Comision Isla de Pascua,* composed of the subsecretaries of the Ministry of Economy, Interior, Education, Foreign Relations, as well as the General Director of Tourism, with Gonzalo Figueroa as the archaeological representative. Henceforth, nothing could be done on the island unless it was first approved by the *Comision.* When there was no consensus, the President of Chile himself would make the final decision. The entire island was decreed to be a national monument.

General Parragué trained a specially selected group of Lan-Chile pilots to make the difficult nine-hour flight to Easter, and some eighty tourists a month landed on the island— to live in tents and to be transported via horseback or truck to the island's unique sites.

In addition, they swam in the green translucent waters of La Pérouse Bay and picnicked on broiled lobster and chilled white wine while Pascuenses in skirts and headpieces of chicken feathers hula-ed and sang songs of their island ancestors. There were sau saus—featuring hunks of roast lamb cooked in earth ovens and served on banana leaves. There was an historic pageant, performed by torchlight. And there were shopping sprees—but with a difference. Every evening, islanders came to the tent camp to sell shell necklaces and wood and stone carvings of birdmen, moai, and replicas of ancient cave stones imbued with mana. Shopping still took the form of bargain barter. One well-carved, foot-high birdman, for example, cost a second-tourist-expedition lady one black brassiere, one drip-dry slip, one pair of woolworth earrings, one half-empty, purse-size bottle of perfume, one box of Band-Aid, one roll-on deodorant.

The wood and stone carvings were the only remains of the ancient island culture still carried on by the modern Pascuenses.

But because of the tourists, other ancient culture elements were revived. Lindblad sent in an expert in Polynesian music who encouraged the islanders to use their indigenous stone drums. He worked with very old people to sort out the ancient Pascuense music, as apart from what was Tahitian, Chilean, or rock-'n'-roll-influenced. Experts in Polynesian dancing were sent in for the same purpose. As for the restoration of ahu and moai, Lindblad put it this way: "Anyone who says the tourists will destroy Easter Island says so because they don't have the slightest idea what the island looks like now—with over 1,000 moai lying around, face down, necks broken. Restoration is a very expensive undertaking. Who is going to put up these things for nobody to see?" Lindblad further pointed out that it was tourism, and perhaps only tourism, which could save the island's unique culture. "Tourism provides the incentive. The tourist—because he's at leisure—goes to see the ancient, the unique. So, for the tourist, we have to revive and restore. Otherwise, why *should* the Easter Islander try to retain the old songs and dances? Why should he build a reed boat when he could have a motor boat? If you 'leave it as it is,' life on Easter Island will eventually become as standardized as it is in the rest of the world. Nobody's going to stay home to make fishhooks out of bone anymore. But people will stay home 'to get cash.' "

Mayor Alfonso Rapu had this to say on the subject, "The impact of tourism on the local traditions will be small compared to the impact of the Chileans living here. And tourists will not only bring money to the island, they may raise the cultural aspirations of the people."

Both men made these statements in 1967. During the following decade, their words proved to be true.

Easter is no longer the most isolated populated spot on earth. The flight from Santiago is now four-and-one-half hours via a Lan-Chile 707 jet (with superior navigation equipment which eliminates the hazardous elements of finding the island). There are two flights a week, one of which goes on to Tahiti and Fiji. The new Matavari Airport Building was constructed in 1970—made from the sides of aluminum trailers left behind when the U.S. Air Force contingent departed.

The plane's arrival is the major social event on the island. Pascuenses gather en masse to greet the tourists. There is, invariably, a contingent of dark-haired girls (with the occasional redhead) decked in the grass skirts and feather headdress worn by their ancestors (with the decorous addition of

Island girls adorned with shells and feathered headpieces and bracelets perform ritual dance as they bid farewell to visitors.

a grass blouse). They sing and dance and, as the visitors descend, other Pascuenses drape the newcomers with shell necklaces. These are for sale—but the next day, the same visitor may be given the necklace as a present. The islanders' generosity to each other spreads over to the tourist. One American schoolteacher who stayed with a Pascuense family reported: "They kept giving me presents. They wouldn't *let* me refuse. They said, 'It's yours because it's ours.' "

Each plane carries freight and mail as well as passengers, and the tourists often find themselves pressed into action as a delivery service while waiting for the plane to depart in Santiago. Hundreds of Pascuenses now live in Chile. There is invariably a continent of them at Pahuel Airport in Santiago where they ask tourists to deliver packages to island relatives (air freight rates being prohibitive). The instant mailmen often find that presenting a package from the mainland is also an open sesame to the hospitality of a Pascuense home.

In 1970, parts of a prefabricated hotel arrived via ship from Miami. It was put up on a cliff overlooking the sea, one mile from town, and it was named The Hango-Roa. (It is part of the Honsa Hotel chain: The "Chilean Hiltons.") A long, low structure it resembles a Florida motel. There are balconies with an ocean view, swimming pool, a lounge, and a bar where tourists and islanders gather in the evening. Each of the sixty rooms has a bath with hot and cold running water. A smaller hotel, the Hotu Matua, lies close to the airport. An average of one hundred tourists a week visit the island.

It is, however, as Mayor Rapu predicted, the Chileans and not the tourists who have brought "civilization" to the island in their diligent drive to Chileanize the Pascuenses. There are TV sets—which play taped programs from Chile. There are radio programs with Chilean news and music. Chilean newspapers are brought in on the jets. All the young people speak

Entrance to the school in Hanga-roa.

fluent Spanish which they learn in school (though they prefer Pascuense at home). And about one-third of the population is Chilean—the mainlanders are attracted to the island by the high-waged work permits.

The houses in Hanga-roa have retained the old style: small, white-washed cinder-blocked, or painted wood, with slanting tin roofs to collect rain water. An ever-increasing number of homes have a TV, a washing machine, and almost all have a radio and a record player (with a collection of South American music, American rock, and new recordings of old songs of their ancestors).

A new school building was constructed in the winter of 1969. It constantly expands in size, as the student population swells. (In 1975, the total island population was 2,000, including 700 Chileans and other continentales. Of this number, there were over 500 schoolchildren. The leading producer was a middle-aged moai-carver who had twenty-four children by his wife and eight more children "on the outside." Youngsters attend classes from the first to the eighth grade, and the school operates in two shifts.

In the evenings, the schoolhouse sometimes doubles as a movie theater. Most popular films are American westerns with Spanish subtitles.

Aside from the addition of a large, wooden moai-faced Madonna and Child—made on the island—the Catholic Church looks just as it did when it was rebuilt in 1958 (with funds donated by the Heyerdahl expedition). The cement-block, whitewashed church has a corrugated iron roof and, inside, is lit by five bare light bulbs hanging from the ceiling. Yet on Sunday mornings, it is immediately transformed into a place of reverence by the ardently enthusiastic voices of the islanders singing hymns in Spanish, Latin—and in Pascuense: melodic, repetitious, and strangely hypnotic songs.

The saddest day in the modern history of the island occurred in January 1969 when the island's most famous and most beloved citizen came home—for the last time. At the age of eighty, Father Sebastian had made his first trip to North America to chaperone a ten-ton moai head which was exhibited in New York City as the start of a fund-raising effort to pay for the raising of more moai.

Father Sebastian appeared on the *Today* show and other radio and television programs. He went to Montreal, to Washington, D.C., and then to New Orleans—where he died of cancer. His body was brought home on a Chilean Air Force plane.

The noted American author, John Dos Passos, attended the funeral. He reported:

> Singing is the natural expression of the Pascuenses. The men and women of the congregation sang the entire burial mass, some of it in Tahitian, which is the church language because Christianity came to them through Tahiti, some in Pascuense. . . . There was no accompaniment. They lifted up their voices and sang their grief. I never attended a burial service where such sincere grief was so beautifully expressed. It didn't sound like any mass we had ever heard.[2]

Father Sebastian was buried beside the grave of Brother Eugène Eyraud. The marble slab above his grave is inscribed:

Reverend Father

SEBASTIAN ENGLERT

CAPUCHIN MISSIONARY

8 January 1969 in His 80th Year

Loved by All

He Lived among Us for 33 Years

He Spoke Our Language

Father Sebastian's fund-raising trip to the United States was sponsored by the International Fund for Monuments. This remarkable one-man, non-profit organization was founded by a former U.S. paratrooper and an engineer, Retired Army Colonel James A. Gray—whose first interest in the matter of monuments was the straightening of the Leaning Tower of Pisa, which is in danger of leaning too far. When the Pisa project was taken over by the Italian government, Colonel Gray, working with one assistant in a small office at 15 Gramercy Park South in New York City, went on to raise all the funds necessary to clean and restore eleven twelfth-century churches carved into the mountainside rock in Lalibela, Ethiopia. This done, he turned his fund-raising attentions to Venice, Italy. He is working with a rubber company to make rubber dikes which will, hopefully, keep that city from sinking). And, in 1968, Colonel Gray took on the massive job of fund-raising for the restoration of ahu, moai and other historic monuments on Easter Island. The work is proceeding under the direction of Dr. William Mulloy, who is not only field director of the Easter Island Committee of the IFM (International Fund for Monuments) but has been given honorary Chilean citizenship.

The island was divided into sections, and restoration work has thus far been confined to the southern section of the triangle.

Important moai and ahu have been restored—with the use of cranes, cement, and other modern conveniences. Among these are *Ahu Akapu,* with its single lonely moai, situated on a high, slender finger of land which juts straight out into the sea. Wrote Mulloy: "The ruins of a modern stone fence extending from the cliffedge and continuing eastward across the ahu plaza had incorporated the statue and pedestal remnants."[4]

According to the islanders, a rongorongo school was once situated here. This was also the place where each new ariki henua (king) was officially installed.

Among the most impressive monuments thus far raised are the five mammoth stone men at Tahai. As they stand staring out over the island—their backs to the sea and the rest of the world—they speak with silent eloquence of the golden age of the statuemakers—and the dark age of destruction which followed—for one of the moai is only a stunted embryo; one was so thoroughly destroyed that only its pedestal remains; two others were partially beheaded, not by time or forces of nature, but by the ancestors of the men who made them.

The two complete giants date from the earliest period when the purse-lipped, hollow-eyed stone men were still squat, stocky, and crudely carved.

The fact that the moai had been toppled from their ahu face down proved to be a fortunate thing so far as preservation of their features was concerned. As Dr. Mulloy noted in one typical case: "The statue . . . was . . . deeply eroded over all of its surface except its face which had been sufficiently buried to have been protected and remained in relatively uneroded condition."[5]

It costs from $1,000 to $5,000 to raise a single moai. Rebuilding an ahu is a more expensive matter: from $20,000 up. Most of the money has been raised by the International Fund for Monuments. Since the funds come entirely from private donations, statue-raising must, perforce, proceed at a slow pace. (The IFM has found that its easiest method of bringing in lump sums is through the sale of life-sized stone and plaster castings of a ten-foot-high moai which comes boxed—for museum or garden use—for $8,000.)

In addition, money for investigations and restorations has come from the National Endowment on the Arts and Humanities, from Chile's National Planning Office, the University of Chile, and the Chilean Bureau of Archives, Libraries and Museums; Lindblad Travel provided funds, vehicles, and personnel. And LAN-Chile and the United States and Chilean air forces gave free transportation for heavy equipment, plus supplies and free tickets for archaeologists and their aides.

As well as restoring ahu and moai—and discovering statues which had been completely buried—the archaeologists have restored *tupa* (towers), caves lined with masonry, walled terraces—and well over half of the unique ceremonial site of Orongo, ranging from a cluster of thirty-three earth ovens (where food was cooked for the participants in the Birdman festivities) to numerous elliptical stone houses in which the island's most important men lived while they waited to see which of them would become Birdman of the Year.

Foreman of the dozen skilled stonemasons who worked on the Orongo site from July through September 1974 was ex-Mayor Alfonso Rapu.

Another aspect of island restoration is the archaeological park which will run from Tahai to Hanga Kio'e (Rat Bay), extending inland for some 500 yards. Not only will the area's many monuments, boat-shaped houses, caves, and so on be restored, but all evidences of modernity—roads, fences—will be eliminated, and the environment will be re-created as it was (according to pollen and soil samples) in prehistoric times, complete with trees and other vegetation which grew there.

Since the archaeological park is near the airport, many tourists who remain only a few hours on the island—as a pause on the flight to Tahiti and Fiji—can at least get a quick look into the island's prehistoric past. And the tourist who settles in on Easter can, in Dr. Mulloy's words "examine the selection of restored monuments as his first activity. He will see a variety of prehistoric sculpture and architecture much as it appeared when it was in use. Information thus acquired will make a decisive difference in his ability to interpret other monuments on the island."[6]

Since Father Sebastian's death, Dr. William Mulloy is acknowledged as the world's foremost expert on Easter Island. On one of his many long-term stays on the island, he became father-in-law to an extremely extended family—for his daughter married a Pascuense. The young couple now live in Wyoming. (Dr. Mulloy will trade places with his son-in-law when he moves to Easter to work full time as the director of restorations.)

On a recent trip to the island, Mulloy arrived with two well-stocked suitcases. He returned carrying only his toothbrush. He had given everything away to his relatives—including the empty suitcases. (There are now some small shops in Hanga-roa and the ECA supplies do not run out—for three supply ships come each year from Chile and other goods are brought in by air freight. Nevertheless, items of clothing and cosmetics—particularly those from the United States—are still highly prized.)

The economy of the island is no longer based on "politeness," or on cigarettes. The appreciation of cash has come to stay. American dollars are particularly favored—for that plane trip to Tahiti, which every Pascuense family seems to be planning. (Dollars are more popular than francs or escudos in Tahiti.)

The island is no longer a vast sheep farm. The American Air Force men exhausted the supply of sheep—by eating them. The cattle population, however, has increased. And there are still three horses for every human on the island. The mares, particularly, run wild, for Pascuenses deem it unlucky to ride one.

Since most of the food is imported from Chile, agriculture has, in the main, died out. But hundreds of fruit trees have been planted, and flourish. Many a schoolchild goes out and picks lunch from the guava bushes or banana trees.

The economy of the island now evolves around fishing and tourism.

Are the Pascuenses happier now that the jets have brought in the outside world, and quick escape from isolation can be bought for the price of a ticket to Tahiti or Santiago?

The young people generally like things the way they are. They have their feet in both worlds. They wear blue jeans; there are some long-haired hippies. They go to the discoteque in the evenings—but their music and dances are not all of the New World. They also play songs of their ancestors, sing them, and dance to them. Young Pascuenses have the sophistication of the New World. But they still have strong identification with the old culture. And they take justifiable pride in the fact that their prehistoric ancestors created on their tiny island one of the most spectacular open-air museums in all the world.

The elderly islanders also, of course, identify strongly with their ancestors, so much so that past often seems like present. They will, for example, recount a story to a visitor as though it happened last week. Later, the visitor may learn that, in fact, the event occurred centuries ago. The old people have reservations about the new life they have been jetted into. One elderly islander expressed it this way, "We are better off now. Our houses have water and electricity. Our children can go to high school in Santiago. We live better. But somehow we have lost something—a sense of community. In the old times, we would have a sau sau that lasted three or four days. Now a sau sau lasts three or four hours. I think we were happier before."

Yet, in the island evenings, the modern world falls away. Even young Pascuenses believe that aku aku still inhabit the land at nighttime—though they can be seen and heard only by islanders, not by Chileans, not by visitors.

But anyone—even the visitor—who climbs the quarry slopes of Rano Raraku at dusk can come close to the ancient world of the statuemakers. The peace which settles over the landscape is like the blanketing of centuries, and the visitor is carried back to the lonely days when the huge stone heads were the sole inhabitants of this place and the only sound was the eternal wash of waves upon the distant cliff-bound shore.

Gabriel Pakarati, an elder of one of the oldest families on the island, stares out over the landscape and into the past. His features are echoed in the profile of an ancient moai.

Bibliographical Reference Notes

CHAPTER ONE:
1. Mulloy, William, "Easter Island," *Natural History,* December 1967, p. 75.
2. *Ibid,* p. 76.

CHAPTER TWO:
1, 2, 3, 4. Roggoveen, M. J.: *Extract from the Official Log of the Voyage of Mynheer Jacob Roggoveen, in the Ships Den Arend, Thienhoven, and De Afrikaanische Galey, in 1721–1722, (insofar as it relates to the discovery of Easter Island: 1722)* Cambridge: Hakluyt Society, 2nd ser., no. 13, 1908.

CHAPTER THREE:
1. Cook, James, *Second Voyage toward the South Pole and Round the World, Performed in the* "Resolution" *and* "Adventure," *1722– 75,* 2 vols. London: W. Strahan and T. Cadell, 1777.
2. Eyraud, Eugene, "Lettre au T.R.P. Superieur General de la Congregation des Sacres-Coeurs de Jesus et de Marie—Valparaiso Decembre 1864," *Annales de la Propagation de la Foi* (Lyon), Vol. 38, 1866.

CHAPTER FOUR:
1. Loti, Pierre, (alias Viaud) "A L'Ile de Pasques," *Cahiers Pierre Loti,* no. 29, Paris: Mars, 1960.
2. Heyerdahl, Thor, *Aku Aku,* New York: Rand McNally, 1958.

CHAPTER FIVE:
1. Loti, Pierre, *A L'Ile de Pasques,* op. cit.
2, 3. Englert, Sebastian, *Island at the Center of the World,* New York: Charles Scribner's Sons, 1970.
4. Forster, G., *A Voyage Round the World in His Britannic Majesty's*

Sloop, Resolution, Commanded by Capt. James Cook, during the Years 1772, 73, 74 and 75, London: W. Strahan and T. Cadell, 1777.

5. Loti, *op. cit.*

CHAPTER SIX:

1, 2. Thomson, W. J., *Te Pito te Henua, or Easter Island,* Report of the U.S. National Museum for the Year Ending June 30, 1889. Washington, D.C.: U.S. Government Printing Office, 1889.

CHAPTER NINE:

1. Smith, Carlyle S., "The Poike Ditch" from *Archeology of Easter Island,* Heyerdahl and Ferdon, eds., Vol. 1, Stockholm: Forum Publishing House, 1961, p. 391.

CHAPTER TEN:

1. Eyraud, Eugene. *Op. cit.*
2. Loti, Pierre. *Op. cit.*

CHAPTER ELEVEN:

1, 3, 4. Englert, Sebastian. *Op. cit.*
2. Thomson, W. J. *Op. cit.*

CHAPTER TWELVE:

1, 3. Métraux, Alfred, *Easter Island; A Stone-age Civilization of the Pacific* (translated by Michael Bullock) London: Andre Deutsch, 1957.
2. Loti, Pierre. *Op. cit.*

CHAPTER THIRTEEN:

1. Métraux, Alfred. *Op. cit.*
2. Unless otherwise indicated all direct quotes in this and the following chapters were obtained by the author in interviews.
3. Englert, Sebastian. *Op. cit.*
4. Mydans, Carl, "Isle of Stone Heads," *Life* Magazine, New York: Time/Life, 1966.

CHAPTER FOURTEEN:

1. Mulloy, William, "The Ceremonial Center of Vinapu," in *Archeology of Easter Island,* Heyerdahl and Fergon, eds., Mon. Sch. of Amer. and Mus. of New Mexico, No. 24, Pt. 1, pp. 93–180. Stockholm: Forum Publishing House, 1961.

CHAPTER FIFTEEN:

1. Métraux, Alfred, *Easter Island; A Stone-age Civilization of the Pacific* (translated by Michael Bullock), London: Andre Deutsch, 1957.

2. Thomson, William J., *Te Pito te Henua or Easter Island,* Washington, D.C.: Rept. U.S. Nat. Mus. for the Year Ending June 30, 1889.

CHAPTER SIXTEEN:

1. LaFay, Howard, "Easter Island and its Mysterious Monuments," *National Geographic Magazine,* Washington, D.C.: National Geographic Society, vol. 121, No. 1, 1962.
2. Dos Passos, John, *Easter Island; Island of Enigmas,* Garden City, New York: Doubleday & Company, Inc., 1971.
3, 4, 5, 6. Mulloy, William, *Preliminary Report of the Restoration of Ahu Huri A Urenga and Two Unnamed Ahu at Hanga Kio'e Easter Island,* New York: Easter Island Committee International Fund for Monuments, Inc., 1973.

Bibliography

Cook, James, *Second Voyage Towards the South Pole and Round the World Performed in the* "Resolution" *and* "Adventure", *1772–75,* 2 vols. London: W. Strahan and T. Cadell, 1777.

Dos Passos, John, *Easter Island; Island of Enigmas.* Garden City, New York: Doubleday & Company, Inc., 1971.

Eiseley, Loren, "The Island of Great Stone Faces," *Holiday,* Philadelphia: Curtis Publishing Company, 1962.

Englert, Sebastian, *Island at the Center of the World; New Light on Easter Island* (translated and edited by William Mulloy). New York: Charles Scribner's Sons, 1970.

Eyraud, Eugène, "Lettre au T. R. P. Superieur General de la Congregation des Sacres-Coeurs de Jesus et de Marie—Valparaiso, Decembre, 1864," *Annales de la Association de la Propagation de la Foi* (Lyon), Vol. 38, 1886, pp. 52–71, 124–138.

Ferdon, Edwin N., Jr., "The Ceremonial Site of Orongo" in *Archeology of Easter Island* (Heyerdahl and Ferdon, eds.), Mon. Sch. of Amer. Res. and Mus. of New Mexico, No. 24, Pt. 1. pp. 221–255. Stockholm: Forum Publishing House, 1961.

Heyerdahl, Thor, and Ferdon, Edwin N., Jr., eds., *Archeology of Easter Island,* No. 24, Pt. 1, 1961. Stockholm: Forum Publishing House, 1961.

Heyerdahl, Thor, *Kon-Tiki,* Chicago: Rand McNally, 1950.

Heyerdahl, Thor, *Aku-Aku,* Chicago: Rand McNally, 1958.

LaFay, Howard, "Easter Island and Its Mysterious Monuments," *National Geographic Magazine.* Washington, D.C.: National Geographic Society, Vol. 121, No. 1, 1962.

Métraux, Alfred, *Easter Island; A Stone-age Civilization of the Pacific* (translated by Michael Bullock). London: Andre Deutsch, 1957.

Mulloy, William, "The Ceremonial Center of Vinapu," in *Archeology of Easter Island* (Heyerdahl and Ferdon, eds.), Mon. Sch. of Amer. and Mus. of New Mexico, No. 24, Pt. 1, pp. 93–180. Stockholm: Forum Publishing House, 1961.

Mulloy, William, "Easter Island," *Natural History,* Vol. 76, No. 10, New York: The American Museum of Natural History, 1967, pp. 74–81.

Mulloy, William, *Preliminary Report of Archeological Field Work, February–July, 1968,* Easter Island, Bulletin 1, New York: Easter Island Committee, International Fund for Monuments, Inc., 1968.

Mulloy, William, *Investigation and Restoration of the Ceremonial Center of Orongo, Easter Island,* Pt. 1, Bull. 4. New York: Easter Island Committee International Fund for Monuments, Inc., 1975.

Mulloy, William, *Preliminary Report of the Restoration of Ahu Huri A Urenga and Two Unnamed Ahu at Hanga Kio'e Easter Island,* New York: Easter Island Committee International Fund for Monuments, Inc., 1973.

Mydans, Carl, "Isle of Stone Heads," *Life* Magazine New York: Time/ Life, 1966.

Palmer, J. L., "A Visit to Easter Island or Rapa Nui in 1868," *Jour. Roy. Geog. Soc.,* Vol. 40. London: 1870, pp. 167–181.

Roggeveen, Jacob, "Extract from the Official Log of Mr. Jacob Roggeveen Relating to His Discovery of Easter Island" in *The Voyage of Captain Don Felipe Gonzalez in the Ship of the Line San Loren-zo with the Frigate* Santa Rosalia *in Company to Easter Island in 1770–71,* pp. 1–24, (translated and edited by Corney, Bolton Glanville) Cambridge: The Hakluyt Society issued for 1903, 1908.

Routledge, Katherine, *The Mystery of Easter Island,* London: Sifton Praed, 1919.

Routledge, Katherine, "The Bird Cult of Easter Island", *Folk-Lore,* Vol. 28, No. 4, pp. 337–355, London: 1917.

Schwartz, Jean-Michel, *New Research on Easter Island: Transportation of the Statues, Deciphering the Rongo-Rongo Writing,* translated by Lowell Bair. New York: Avon Books, 1975.

Skjölsvold, Arne, "The Stone Statues and Quarries of Rano Raraku", in *Archeology of Easter Island* (Heyerdahl and Ferdon, eds.), Stockholm: Forum Publishing House, pp. 339–379.

Thomson, William J., *Te Pito te Henua or Easter Island,* Washington, D.C.: Rept. U.S. Nat. Mus. for the year ending June 30, 1889.

Index